# Sometimes I Feel Like a Nut

**Also by Jill Kargman**

Fiction

*Arm Candy*

*The Ex–Mrs. Hedgefund*

*Momzillas*

*Wolves in Chic Clothing: A Novel* (with Carrie Karasyov)

*The Right Address: A Novel* (with Carrie Karasyov)

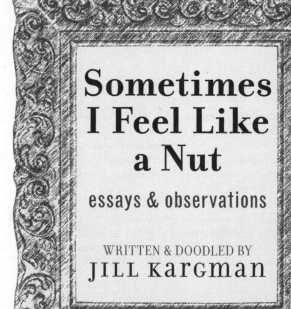

# Sometimes I Feel Like a Nut

## essays & observations

WRITTEN & DOODLED BY
### JILL KARGMAN

WILLIAM MORROW
*An Imprint of HarperCollinsPublishers*

The names of certain individuals have been changed to protect their privacy.

HarperCollins books may be purchased for educational, business, or sales promotional use. For information please write: Special Markets Department, HarperCollins Publishers, 10 East 53rd Street, New York, NY 10022.

FIRST EDITION

Library of Congress Cataloging-in-Publication Data

Kargman, Jill, 1974–
  Sometimes I feel like a nut : essays and observations / written and doodled by Jill Kargman. — 1st ed.
     p. cm.
  ISBN 978-0-06-200719-3
  I. Title.
  PS3611.A783S66 2011
  814'.6—dc22

                                                              2010043480

11  12  13  14  15   OV/RRD   10 9 8 7 6 5 4 3

Dedicated, with non-stalkerish admiration,

to

Woody Allen,

my hero and the funniest human ever

# Contents

# Introduction

The irony is I fucking hate coconut. As in full vomitorious spine chills just thinking about its nasty texture, to say nothing of the chunder-taunting scent that conjures peroxide-y sluts smearing their 'kini cleaves with Panama Jack "tanfastic" oil. I might even go so far as to say I don't even trust people who like coconut. But still, despite nightmarish Hawaiian Tropic/*Girls Gone Wild* visions and hellacious flashbacks of a bearded Tom Hanks looking not unlike the twentieth hijacker eating coconuts on that island, if I had to identify myself with one advertising campaign, it would be the eighties jingle of Mounds and Almond Joy. Sometimes you feel like a nut, sometimes you don't.

For twenty-five years, my father worked for Doyle Dane Bernbach, the legendary Madison Avenue advertising agency that was proto–Don Draper, complete with the same martini lunches and genius minds, but the Jewy Jewstein version. When most peeps see commercials, they get up to pee, get another soda, or comment on the program that was just interrupted. Yeah, no. Not in our house. "Be quiet," my dad would instruct us through the first decade of my childhood. "Guys, shhhh, please, the commercials are on."

He was obsessed, so we were obsessed. Copywriting. Casting. Execution. We raved about great ads and rolled our eyes over the shitty ones. I still do (Dr. Scholl's "Ya Gellin'," anyone?). I started to think of individuals in terms of campaigns. The blow job queen was Bounty ("The Quicker Picker-Upper"), the geeks who got hazed in high school were Timex ("Takes a Licking and Keeps on Ticking"), the virginal church mouse was Ivory soap ("99.44% Pure"), the hot guy I had a crush on was Bell telephone ("Reach Out and Touch Someone"—i.e., *me*).

My brother and I grew up so attuned to branding and media images that when it came time to write my college essay, to, in fact, brand myself, I chose to do so with a slogan. At the time, fall of 1991, HBO's tagline was "Simply the Best." AT&T's was "The Right Choice." I could have kissed ass and picked one of those and sold myself in a shining halo of light as the girl upon whose blessed head they should bestow admission. But I am a firm believer in truth in advertising. So while I could have tooted my horn and painted myself as my public persona of well-rounded student, a capella singer, newspaper editor, big brag sheet blah blah blah, the reality was—and still is—that I'm a weirdo. I'm inappropriate. I laugh when I'm not supposed to (actress in a play accidentally falling off the stage, funerals), and I peed my pants a little bit when my poor French waiter tried his damndest to recite the "made in de haus ice cream flavors" as "bitch and apricunt." I laugh all day long, pretty much. I can't not laugh. Humor has been the buoy that keeps my entire family afloat.

My dad did stand-up comedy to put himself through business school and he instilled in us a value system based on good times and cackles aplenty. Not the let's-dance-on-tables-and-snort-lines-of-coke type of good times, but let's laugh our asses off if we can. We're all gonna be dead in eighty years or less, and the ones who live the best obviously aren't the ones with the most money or most successful careers; they're the ones who laugh the most. Who are the most nutty. Not as in wack-job serial killer who makes suits out of fat people, but as in the right kind of bonkers. The goofy kind. The type who giggles and guffaws, even in tricky times.

My idol, Woody Allen, once had a character in one of his films hatch a formula I value above anything Einstein could have cracked: Comedy = Tragedy + Time.

Brilliant, right? The bigger the tragedy, the more time is needed, obviously (remember when everyone went shithouse when the *New York Post* used "H'caust" in a headline to abbreviate "Holocaust"?!). And obviously big tragedies can't ever become comedic. The little blind panhandling child in *Slumdog Millionaire* won't sit around at age ninety-two and be like, "*Ha,* wasn't that so funny how those beggar pimps poured acid in my retinas?" But in general, my 20/20 hindsight has made me, eventually, absolutely *howl* at anything on the spectrum, from the ordinary, Seinfeldian banal ("That's gold, Jerry, gold!") to situations that were, at the time, unbearable. Granted, my life is a slice of cheesecake relative to what some endure (*Slumdog Millionaire* chemically burnt eyeballs et al.); I was hardly shaking a cup on the corner, I've never buried parents, and my New Yorker frenzied "stress" of being a working mom of three was always relative. But I did get cancer at thirty-five. And the surgery gave me scars that make me look not unlike stitched-up Sally from Tim Burton's *The Nightmare Before Christmas*. But, honestly, in comparison to some past romantic breakups and other previous life drama, the C-word was nada mucho. (BTW, the C-word used to be not "cunt" but "cobbler," a term I detest because it's a fruit dessert *and* someone who fixes shoes; go figure.)

Because I've trained myself to use nuttiness as a coping mechanism, the surgeons at Sloan-Kettering were quasi-uncomfy with my O.R. Tumor Humor ("So am I totally gonna be Sinéad O'Kargman or what?"). But when I e-mailed my friends updates and wisecracks about my wheelchair drag racing, they all said they were happy to see I was still joking around. That I was still myself, still a nut. I think in my little abacus of smiles, I'm racking up more than most. I'm hoping that anyone who may be in a quagmire might recognize themselves in some of these bizarre adventures and know that, in time, as St. Woody of Allen said, they will be mined for comedy. More than comedy. Gold, Jerry, gold.

 JK

# Sometimes I Feel Like a Nut

# Glossary

**after party:** I do not know what this is. Must be in PJs
and 'zontal by Jon Stewart or eyelids are at half-mast
and "beeyotch" takes on new meaning.

**food baby:** When you eat such a huge meal you look
pregnant—but instead of the tenant being a fetus, it's
eggplant Parm.

**Frederica Bimmel:** The size-14 murder victim whose
skin Buffalo Bill fashions into a suit in *The Silence
of the Lambs.* As in: *OMG, I can't believe we ate those
cheese fries at that hour; I'm Frederica Bimmel.*

**godfathering:** Having heavy days of your period, i.e.,
blood everywhere. As in: *We can have sex tonight, but
I'm totally godfathering so the bedsheet will make the*
Law & Order *sound when we finish.*

**jam-jim:** Ladino word my mother uses to mean "the sound in a mosque," i.e., silence. For example: *We went to this new restaurant that was supposed to be happenin' but when we went in, it was totally jam-jim.*

**kielbasa fingers:** When you chow too much MSG and your rings are cutting off circulation. For instance: *OMG, we totally feasted at China Fun and this morning I have total kielbasa fingers.* Synonym: "soy-raped."

**maror:** Bitter herb in Passover Seder but used colloquially, as in, *That girl is always complaining; why is she so fucking maror?*

**matando moshcas:** Ladino expression: killing flies, like when someone has nothing to do. E.g.: *Poor department stores in this economic crisis! I walked into Bendel's and the salespeople were matando moshcas!*

**quahog:** Giant North Atlantic clam, i.e., megabitch. *That girl always looks like she just sucked a lemon; I hear she's a total quahog.*

**Sistine baby:** A little nugget so cute s/he looks chiseled off an Italian frescoed ceiling.

**Spitzering:** Bangin' hos. Oh, sorry, "courtesans." Like, *They seem like a really cute couple but I hear he's totally Spitzering.*

**tramp stamp:** Tattoo just above your ass crack.

**wait up, guys:** A certain type of social climber whose identity is wrapped up in running with those s/he deems "popular." As in: *Wait up, guys, what're you doing? Oh, after party at the Boom Boom Room? Wait up!*

## WORDS I WANT TO BRING BACK INTO HEAVY ROTATION

**crummy:** I never knew it was spelled with two *m*'s and not like "crumby," like something that instantly disintegrated into crumbs. But no, it's "crummy." And I love it. See "lousy."

**golly:** I use "OMG" a lot but now that it's been co-opted by Miley and the gang, I want to revert to the Pollyanna version. Especially after I e-mailed my mom "OMFG" and she was unpleased.

**lousy:** My dad always says it when food tastes like shit and I think it's really ol' school and funny.

**rascal:** Mischief without evil. Bad kids today seem like
they're lighting shit on fire.

**robber:** I feel like kids today don't fear "robbers" the
way my brother and I did, seventies-style, like the
Hamburglar with the Zorro mask and shit.

## WORDS I WANT TO NEVER HEAR AGAIN

**cobbler:** See above.

**custard:** Dunno why, just sounds mucusy. I'm big on
texture.

**guesstimate:** My friend Lisa's personal cheese-grater-to-
the-ear, and as with things that irk close friends, it's
contagious. Fuck "guesstimate." You can totally see
the person who came up with it feeling so clever, like
whoever invented "Hotlanta." Which isn't even clever
'cause it doesn't rhyme! I would like to rename it
"Fatlanta."

**"I have a salmon special for $19.95":** Double whammy.
I hate when waiters say "I have" (you don't "have"
anything, you're just fucking bringing it out). Also
not into when they give the price. Unless it's some

serious gouging, like white truffles or lobster flown in from a private Richard Branson–y island off the coast of Maine and you're paying for the airfare. With little lobster seat belts.

**nother:** As in *That's a whole nother thing.* "Nother" is not a word, people!

# 2

# Things That Haunt Me

I don't freak about heights. Or Freddy Krueger. Or snakes. In fact, when my husband, Harry, and I drove cross-country—sorry, he drove cross-country and I sat managing the pre-XM staticky terrestrial radio stations—we stopped in a small town in rural Wyoming. Wait, that was a redundancy. After a lunch of something fried, we saw a dude with a huge python wrapped around his entire body. When I exclaimed how cool it was he asked me if I wanted to try it on.

"Totally!" I said, as Harry's face contorted in sheer shock.

"Who are you?" Harry asked me, unable to reconcile that the girl who shrieks at ear-splitting decibels at the sight of a bug was now Britneying a mammoth reptile.

I may scream over a roach on the sidewalk—oh, sorry, water bug (but let's face it, they're all fucking roaches)—but a nine-foot anaconda's *pas de problème*. Which is all to say: I am a freakazoid about fear. I don't get scared of regular things that have the word "phobia" attached (arachnophobia, acrophobia, etc.). The things that haunt me are sometimes understandable but still pretty abnormal. Here's some backstory on a few assorted things I find extremely troubling.

## 1. VANS

Yes, vans. Not the sk8er checkerboard Ked-like SoCal shoe, but rather the vehicle. I hereby propose the following: nothing good comes from vans. I'm not talking about old Volkswagen hippie vans filled with pot smoke or even ones where you can see the band equipment piled in. I'm talking windowless, double-door, *Silence of the Lambs*–mobiles. I'm talking duct-taped Frederica Bimmel in the back. I'm talking drug dealers. I have long believed vans almost always hold kidnapped kids. When I was a child in the seventies in New York, the tragedy of Etan

Patz, a little boy who disappeared on his way to school, haunted the city. Haunted. I mean every parent on every block told their kids the story, how he vanished the first time his dad let him walk alone. For years I'd look at creepy vans and assume a kid was stuck in there with rope around him, trying to force out a sound from under the silver tape or bandana shoved in his mouth. Buffalo Bill's escapades in *The Silence of the Lambs,* among those of other Hollywood villains, included the use of vans, further supporting my theory. Then, in college, the worst story. As in, please dive into my nightmares, the water's warm. I met a girl from rural Vermont who was so sweet. One night we stayed up talking about her new boyfriend and I asked if they'd done it yet. She told me they were waiting and I wondered why, as they seemed so cute and happy together. And then she told me that when she was fourteen she was walking home from a neighbor's house when a *van* pulled up alongside her, the door slid open, and three guys grabbed her, threw her inside, and gang-raped her virginity away. I almost threw up. I was ass-white. I was a *mess*. But natch it only added to my anxiety about vans, which has spiraled to traumatic proportions.

Then years later, yours truly decided to take a driving lesson. Yes, at thirty-five I do not drive. Long story long, I'd never needed to drive before, what with buses and taxis and N trains and, you know, legs. But I'd grown tired of everyone teasing me and decided that my lack of motor vehicle knowledge was not in sync with the fact that I am a strong independent woman. Whoops, sorry, that sounded way too Beyoncé-esque. I just felt like it wasn't part of my personality to be a perma-passenger. After all, as Volkswagen ads say, on the road of life, there are passengers and there are drivers. Okay, fine, so I couldn't drive, but I felt like I was a driver type, despite the sad fact that I truly did not know which pedal was which.

My teacher Dennis was the local high school football coach near my parents' house in Massachusetts.

At first I was positively schvitzing, convinced I'd mow over an ice-cream-licking tot or golden retriever named Bailey or Tucker, but then my years of playing Atari Pole Position kicked in. (I knew they were good for something! Now I just have to figure out how the hell Donkey Kong helped me . . .) My fear subsided and I got really into it.

After my first lesson I thought I was Mario Andretti. Dennis said I was an A student!

The more curves the road took, the more empowered and revved up I felt, until by the hour's end I was ready to do a full Whitesnake-era Tawny Kitaen hood-straddle. But since I lacked a dry-ice machine for smoky effects, flame-red waist-length hair, and a gauzy dress, I decided against it. Oh, and also, instead of a white Jaguar my chariot was a beige Ford Focus emblazoned with the words "Student Driver." Decidedly less scorching hot.

As it turned out, however, my cockiness was all beginner's luck. Clichés exist for a reason, and that reason is me. My second lesson *blew* and left me with zero confidence at the wheel, which I am plagued with at this printing.

What, you may ask, does this have to do with vans? Everything, actually. So lesson #2: I'm cruising along trying to keep my focus in the Focus, basking in the rays of my instructor's praise of my killa skills, feeling extra Tawnyish. *Then,* lo and behold, a ramshackle death trap on wheels (*van*) cuts me off with a crazy rubber-burning screeching turn in front of me. I *scream* my head off, slamming on the brakes, and if my harrowing escape isn't enough for a second-day driving student, suddenly the double door that would usually hold the roped up kidnap-pee with duct-taped piehole, unable to scream, *burst open,* unleashing a fury of splattered food. Dennis leaned over and slammed my horn until the asshole van driver clued in that his vehicle had just shat out a seafood feast. As it turns out, assholic driver was not a serial killer, but in fact a moronic caterer en route to a deliver a Silence of the Clams beachside lobster bake. Not one, not two, but about twenty red crustaceans and bags o' steamers littered the road and a huge bowl of gloppy potato salad landed on the hood of my car. So I had slammed on the brakes and swerved out of the way, deftly avoiding claw crackage, crossing over the double yellow line. Thank almighty Adonai there wasn't an oncoming car careening toward us or yours truly would've gone the way of the aforementioned crustaceans. After hyperventilation that nearly necessitated a brown paper bag, I shakily attempted some parallel parking but was so rattled by the onslaught of flying sea creatures that I lost my nerve and my will to keep trying to drive. Again.

Which is all to say: fuck vans.

## 2. NELLIE OLESON

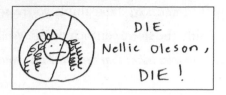

I'm still haunted, twenty-five years later, by my *fierce, all-consuming, intense* loathing of the ringleted *Little House on the Prairie* cunty villainess. Her smug smirk. Her ice-blue eyes. Her merciless taunting of Laura Ingalls, who, while beaverish and semi-annoying, did not deserve that shit. Nellie had her petticoats and her satin bows and her big-ass house: she'd won! Her family owned the fucking store! Everyone else had to cross fields swinging empty buckets to score their loot and she just rolled out of her princess bed downstairs! Bitch. She had it all; why did she need to goad Laura with those bitchy dirty looks and snobbery? As a child I hated her *so* much I literally wanted to go and find the actress who played her and murder her and chop off her blond curls. Because you can't act evil that well. It's like Brenda on *90210* years later. But way worse. 'Cause Nellie never cracked. My other fantasy involving

N.O. was to take a time machine back there and show her all my stuff, like my TV, and say, "You think you're so great with your pa owning the store, you rich bitch? Well look what I got! *A fucking television, that's what! Fuck you, Nellie Oleson!*"

## 3. MEAT

Okay, I know what you're thinking: ew, she's a righteous vegetarian. No, no, I'm not. I swear. In fact I'm eating a chicken burger as I write this. Not really, but I will later. Animal rights is just not a cause I think about (sorry). Boo-hoo, I like my lipstick and medicine. I wear leather. Kill the cow to make my boots, I don't care, but I just don't really want to eat it. Here's why.

When I was twelve, I wanted to have sex sooo badly. I know, that's, like, way too young north of the Mason-Dixon but I was *so* curious and I wanted to close my eyes and moan like the girls in the movies 'cause it felt so good. Little did I know it would fucking kill, but more on that later. This relates to cows because I was having a major flirtfest with my friend Jessica's Camp Weekela friend

Owen. My best friend, Dana, and I shopped camps and the Weekela guy did a whole presentation and said earnestly, "This is the Rolls-Royce of camps." Our parents decided we should hit the Chevy of camps instead. But once I saw the gorgeous guys from Jessica's camp pictures I wished we'd passed on Like a Rock and instead requested some Grey Poupon.

Fast-forward a couple months and Owen was attending Jessica's coed slumber party. Tween sparks flew. I knew Owen and I would be playing tonsil hockey big-time. I secretly plotted maybe even letting him go to second. Which at the time, back in '87, was boobs, not beedges or whatever the fuck rainbow kissing/Cleveland steamer/ Dirty Sanchez fast-lane shit "yutes" do today. So on the night of what was to be the first real make-out session of my life, some idiot at the party decided we should pop *The Texas Chainsaw Massacre Part 2* into the Betamax. In case you haven't suffered the misfortune of enduring this silver screen gem, it opens with a chili contest where the main ingredient in the blue-ribbon-winning concoction is . . . (drumroll) . . . people. Yum! I didn't feel so hot. In fact, I began to feel my chunder mid-esophagus. I then proceeded to toss my tacos all night, sending Owen fleeing, and the only thing I had my arms around for the rest of the evening was the porcelain shrine of misery. I came home the next day vowing never to eat red meat again.

My mom crossed her arms. "You're kidding me! I just bought steaks," she said, pissed. "Can't you become a vegetarian tomorrow?"

My parents thought it was just a phase but to this day I do not eat moo or bahhh. Or oink, for that matter. I know, I know, the piggy lobby says it's "The Other White Meat," but bacon looks fuckin' red to me. I'm sure real vegetarians think my grilled slabs of fowl are foul but somehow I'm not as grossed out by bird. And now I'm anemic. Thanks, Wes Craven. Or whoever the hell ruined my cute-boy mackfest. I'm now the loser at the wedding who subtly asks the caterer if there's a veggie plate and is greeted with some boiled carrots rolling around. And my iron levels are so in the shitter I whack my leg on a stray toy car and have a bruise the color of a J.Crew navy cardigan. God damn you, cannibal chili cook!

## 4. MIMES AND CLOWNS

Now, I know I'm definitely insulting the Canadians, who are the host country of the foremost clown college and pinnacle of the clowning arts as the birthplace of Cirque du So Lame. I know that miming and clowning are two very distinct "arts." But I'm just gonna fucking lump them together anyway! What, like I'm scared they're gonna come after me? Well, yes, actually. Yes, I am. Once again images from television and film haunted me for my formative years. Maybe this is a pattern linking my fears to rape, but actually I first learned what rape was from an episode of the aforementioned *Little House* where a lowlife clown from a traveling circus raped some girl in a barn. The thing about both is that usually they are male and wear makeup, which in itself weirds my ass out. Trust me, I love me a glam tranny, lashes and lipstick, but somehow it's the caricatured faces painted on that are cause for alarm. For example, a clown or mime rapist can have a growly sex face on but over it is a biiiiig happy smile painted on. So creepy. Like, beyond. I can't handle it.

Mimes freak me out because I'm so talkative that the mute thing alone wigs me out. I loved the scene in *Tootsie* where Dustin Hoffman is all depressed missing Jessica Lange and is strolling through Central Park and sees a mime and just fucking pushes him down. Growing up there were always mimes in Central Park. It was like what hippies are to San Francisco children: loathsome. The king of all mimes, of course, was Marcel Marceau.

My dad was traveling on the now-defunct Concorde on a business trip. He is so not a fame fucker and is always clueless about celebs, but I got in the habit of asking him who he sat next to on those flights because it was almost always someone famous. Once he sat next to "this rock star guy" who he said was named "Stung." It was Sting. Another time Michael Jackson was in front of him, *avec* entourage. Countless actors, models, designers. My dad didn't know exactly who they were so I had to grill him on roles in movies until he'd be like, "Oh yeah! That one! The gal who boiled the rabbit in that movie with Michael Douglas!"

Then one day he comes home and says he sat next to, of all the glamorous passengers in the world, mime royalty: Marcel Marceau. Who ironically talked my dad's ear off *THE ENTIRE FLIGHT.* He also ate a meal whose main ingredient was apparently raw cloves of garlic and proceeded to breathe a brown cloud of stink over my poor father for hours and hours. My dad sat and nodded, nostrils flared in horror, as he thought to himself, AREN'T YOU SUPPOSED TO BE A FUCKING MIME?!

Typical. See, like a priest who butt-fucks little boys, anything extreme is prone to snap in the other direction. No talking allowed in your profession? Then you won't shut up!

As for clowns, same deal. If you have to be 100 percent cheery and smiley *ALL. THE. FUCKING. TIME.,* then you probably are kind of a dick. You know how your friend who scooped ice cream that stoner summer at Rocky Mountain Chocolate Factory still can't look at banana fudge ripple after so many binges? My theory is that it's like that for people, like clowns, who have to be so damn perky all the time. They are allergic to perk offstage. Year after year there are new images of scary clowns. The

Matthew Barney creepy clowns also played into my fears, as did random police blotter mentions of routine armed robberies by clowns, and even Chucky, which was a doll and not a clown but carried the same idea of innocence that was corrupted and brutal and knife wielding. Funnily enough, I had made a conscious effort not to pass on this fear as I know it's bizarre and could hamper my kids' birthday party experiences. But no such luck. Without a word from me, my younger daughter, Ivy, froze at a party when Silly Billy yelled at her three-year-old self for whispering with her friend instead of paying attention to His Majesty's balloon-twisting antics. In tears, she left the kiddies' pit around him and retreated to the sofa safety of her mom's lap. My friend Marcie then tried to comfort her when Silly Billy turned and snapped at us to STFU.

"Gee," Marcie said. "I've never been bitched out by a clown before."

I subsequently learned that Billy and his family were the subjects of the documentary *Capturing the Friedmans,* and that allegedly Silly Billy's brother, another clown, was a child molester. Good times! When on occasion I have to stomach the circus, it's not the lion and tigers and tightrope and trapeze and motorcycle guy in a Globe of Death that freak me out. It's the clowns. If I never see a big red shoe again it'll be a blessing. I also wonder if all those clown rapists wore squeaky red noses during the rape. Like the victim could reach up and honk it for help. Food for thought. Cotton candy and yellow popcorn. Vomit.

# 3

# Babysitters from Hizznell

The revolving door of my childhood sitters began to spin in the late seventies, when my mother, who cooked, cleaned, and took care of us by herself, decided to get some extra help and put an ad on the bulletin board at Juilliard and the School of American Ballet. It was before they built the sleek new dorm the two schools now share at Lincoln Center and many gifted kids from around the country couldn't matriculate if they couldn't find housing in New York. So I spent my whole childhood with an au pair living with us, along with her flute or toe shoes.

The first was Ann. With thighs you could floss your teeth with, the Jamaican-by-way-of-Liverpool Brit was a gorgeous dancer who lived in the small room upstairs and babysat my brother, Willie, and me when she wasn't studying. My mom recalls her as elegant and sweet, a nice person to have around and a hard worker. There was just one small problem. She put the "Ann" in "anorexia." When we brought her on a ski trip to Idaho, and Willie and I were in ski school, she decided to sweat off the carrot she'd eaten in the scalding Jacuzzi. For four hours.

My parents were skiing down to the base when they spied the blackboard by the chairlift at the bottom. In large chalk letters it read: COCO AND ARIE KOPELMAN: CALL LODGE ASAP! Panic. They had no clue what had gone down—was Willie neck-braced in one of those ski patrol sleds? Had I choked on a tater tot in the kiddie mountain cafeteria? They raced to the courtesy phone. Ann had passed out. Unconscious post-soakage in 104-degree bubbles. She'd been spatula'd off the tiles and luckily made a full recovery. But this was only the beginning of the chaos.

When we got back to New York, my parents decided to repaint the apartment, and they were under contract to use the company the building recommended. My mom took me to an interview for kindergarten (yes, this is normal in New York) as tarps were laid out and paint poured in pans.

Cut to my dad at the office with one of his biggest

clients, a Midwestern fat cat hailing from a rectangular-shaped red state. Mid-schmooze and presentation, his secretary came in with a worried look.

"Mr. Kopelman?"

"We're in the middle of an important meeting," he explained.

She stood nervously in the doorway. "Um, it's your sitter."

He looked concerned.

"Excuse me for one moment," he said apologetically, rising to take the call outside.

"*Mr. Kopelman!*" Ann screamed into the phone in her English accent.

"Ann, what's wrong? Are the kids okay?"

"The children are fine—" she sputtered between gasps.

"Okay, what's wrong?!" he asked.

*"THE PAINTER IS TRYING TO RAPE ME!"*

"What?!"

"The painter! He's trying to *rape me*."

*Gulp.* Holy shit.

"Where are you now?" my dad asked, trying to remain calm.

"I've locked myself in your bathroom with a carving knife!" she wailed, her voice quivering.

My dad swallowed hard. Fuck.

"I'm on my way."

As he grabbed his coat, he went sheepishly to face his client.

"I-I'm terribly sorry," he stammered. "But I have an emergency."

"Everything okay?" the midwesterner from Purina Cat Chow inquired.

"No, unfortunately. I'm afraid I have to go," my dad replied. "My painter is raping my babysitter."

The client shook his head. "Only in New York."

After sprinting home fifteen blocks, my dad busted open the door to find the painter had bailed and Ann was crouched and sobbing with a hunter-green handprint on her boob and the thigh of her jeans. Ladies and gentlemen of the jury, exhibits A and B. She was a mess. Bawling. My mom and I came home to complete chaos and my parents called the painting company, freaking out.

"She's lyin'," the owner said to my mother. "You should see what goes down with my guys. You should *see*! I got ladies up and down Park Avenue callin' for painters. They open the door in the nude. Buck nekkid."

Ew. My mom tried to shake the image of some rich matron trying to toss a Benjamin Moore–covered roller aside and throwing the Polish painter on her Léron linens, untying her Pratesi robe, and unhooking his overalls.

"Perhaps, but that's not what happened here," my mother asserted. "She had green paw prints all over her clothes."

"She prolly came on to him. They always do."

No apologies, nothing.

The next day came the wrath of Ann's six-foot-five Rasta boyfriend pacing our living room like a caged panther, gripping his dreadlock-covered head as if he had a migraine that would make his whole noggin explode onto our carpet, covering our shellacked walls with his brain's bloody mist.

*"I'M GONNA FOOKIN' KEEL HEEM! HE IS A DEAD MON! I'M GONNA FOOKIN KEEL HEEM!"* he screamed. *"GEEVE ME HEEZ NAME! HE IS A DEAD MON. HE. IS. A. DEAD. MON."*

"Okay, calm down . . . ," my dad begged, attempting to soothe the sheer unbridled ire that was the nuclear mushroom cloud erupting in the living room. "Killing him does what? Then you go to jail and you can't see Ann anymore. Then your life is ruined. What good does that do?"

Her boyfriend channeled his extreme rage into deep breaths that morphed into hyperventilation.

*"Geeve me his name!"* he yelled. For the record, it was Rudy.

"It's not worth it," my dad continued. This went on for another hour until my parents had a promise from Ann's boyfriend he'd drop it and not track this guy's ass down and machete him to Polish pieces.

"What a day," my mom said with a sigh after the mollified couple had left. "How is this our life? We spent the whole afternoon talking this Rastafarian out of committing murder."

Shortly after her near-ravaging, Ann's studies ended. It was time for a clean start.

Enter Sue. Her hair was blond, her sweet home Alabama. With huge blue eyes and a virginal demeanor, my parents were thrilled when she smiled in the doorway for the interview. They spoke with her twang-talkin' warm, kind parents, who sent them homemade jams, and she happily installed herself in Ann's old room.

It started out okay. She was very sweet, and seemed to be happy in potentially overwhelming New York and not longing too much for the calmer pace of the Deep South. But there was one small detail that hadn't come up in the Q & A session she'd had with my parents. She was a sex fiend.

The first evidence of this was when a neighbor called my parents.

"I'm . . . afraid my maid has witnessed some inappropriate behavior by your babysitter," she confessed.

Huh? Sue? Southern belle Sue?

The neighbor arranged a sit-down between my parents and her nervous maid, who recounted how one evening as she was drawing the curtains by her window, which looked out on our building's roof, she saw little Sue running about stark naked, giggling and being chased by a large black man.

"I'm the Big Bad Wolf!" he bellowed as she ran from his grasp, laughing.

"What are you gonna do to me, Big Bad Wolf?"

"The Big Bad Wolf is gonna fuck your brains out!" They ran in circles as the maid crossed herself in the window and called her boss right away.

My parents gulped. Time to talk with Sue.

"Um, Sue, you can't bring men into this building. This is a co-op and we have very strict rules about guests."

"I'm sorry!" she cried, weeping. "Pleeeeeeease don't tell my parents! *Pleeeeease!*"

My parents looked at each other.

"I won't do it again, I *promise*," she swore.

A few weeks later, my mom brought me home from school, and from the second we got off the elevator, she smelled the stench. "PU!" I recalled her saying. (Remember that? What happened to PU? And what did it stand for? Random.) Within seconds, Willie emerged. He was matted with sweat and waddling in a T-shirt and a bulging diaper that contained heaps of what we call in Latin *rhea explosiva*.

"Oh my god," my mom exclaimed, scooping up her little son. "*Sue?* SUUUUUUUE!"

My mom's voice rang through the apartment. Clearly Willie had been majorly neglected, considering he was coated in perspiration and poo. "SUE! SUE?" We followed my mom as she looked for her. Willie's nursery. Nope. The bathroom. No. My room? Nada. Nowhere to be found. She walked down the hallway and saw the door to the den was closed. Just as my mom reached for the doorknob, Sue opened the door with a startled look on her face and her bra showing through her half-buttoned shirt. My mom pushed the door open and there was our doorman, Joe, sans uniform top, zipping the fly of his gray pants with the gold stripe down the side. It was unclear where the doorman hat was. Maybe Sue wore it with nothing else as they porked.

Willie and I stood with wide eyes as my mom asked Joe to please leave and told Sue there was going to be a Talk that evening.

"Pleeeeease don't tell my parents!" Sue said beseechingly.

"I thought I told you this is not acceptable!" my dad said.

"You said I couldn't bring in people from outside the building," she said between tears in her defense. "So I found someone in the building."

After a last warning my pushover parents acquiesced to her pleas and let her stay. But the worst was yet to come.

Sue's pal Nightingale was trouble. She was a tall, striking brunette with that disco-era big hair worn with two combs. I liked her because she always came over after my parents left and would bring us frozen Kit Kat bars. As Sue and Nightingale watched our cracked-out shit-eating grins as we tore off the dark orange paper and foil wrappers, they realized something. Chocolate = kiddie currency. With those four cocoa-dipped bars, they could buy our silence.

Nightingale had wads of money. Why? Because rather than work for peanuts as an au pair wiping asses, she worked two blocks from our apartment, at the Playboy Club on Fifth Avenue and Sixty-seventh Street, a huge mansion that is now the Polish embassy. But in the 1970s, it housed a different genre of poles.

Bunny suits with cotton tails paraded by the cabaret tables serving cocktails on logo-covered napkins. Somehow I knew what Playboy was even at age five because of its extensive advertising campaigns for subscriptions. Because I was glued to my television, particularly the commercials, the bow-tied rabbit was already burned in my brain. Nightingale told Sue she could easily get her cute self a gig there as well, and so soon Willie and I began our career as child extortionists, bribed with Kit Kats for our silence. Nightingale would come over, help Sue put coats over our footie pajamas, and take us to the Playboy Club. Sue installed us in a back room, a lounge for the girls, with a VHS tape of *Flash Gordon* and our chocolate. She would make the rounds with Nightingale and come in every few minutes to check on us.

It worked out great! She got her extra dough and we got candy and movies on a school night; bingo!

When my parents needed her on a night she had to work, we'd simply come along for the ride. This happened once a week for about two months, but it felt like we rode the Hefner Express for ages.

And then one night the blackmail train came to a screeching halt.

My parents left for a dinner party and arrived at the hostess's home to discover that her husband had abruptly fallen ill and the party was canceled. As it was the dead of winter and they didn't much feel like going out anyway, they decided to come home.

When we walked in laughing, me on Nightingale's shoulders and Willie piggyback on Sue, our giggles quickly turned to busted sheepish grimaces. I think I recall Nightingale cursing as we all four beheld the *ENRAGED* red-faced gazes of my parents on the foyer bench.

And that was the end of Sue. They had her packing her bags before you could sing the chorus of "Centerfold."

Many others followed: Sabina, the morbidly obese German cellist, who was such a compulsive eater she once ate a dinner my mom had prepared for eight guests. Sabina thought it was food up for grabs and Dysoned it all down, leaving my mom sobbing in her bathrobe as she found the empty platters with her dinner party starting in a half hour. *Buh-bye,* Sabina.

Saadia from Morocco: she lasted for a while and I remember her screaming and beating her chest when Sadat was assassinated. Eventually she was gonzo, too. There was the gal who had a life-consuming obsession with the Doobie Brothers, covering the walls with posters. And there was scary Lucille. I asked Lucille if I should go ring for the elevator since we were headed to the park. Her response to my first-grade self? "No. Don't get the elevator! Why don't we all just spread our wings and jump out the window and fly down!" Sarcasm + six-year-old = massive confusion and in this case, fear.

In the end, while this chorus of artistically talented but high-maintenance women was more trouble than it was worth, I'm glad I was exposed to the colorful chaos, but as we got older, the (sometimes graphic) book was finally closed on the student au pairs, a permanent wedge stuck in the revolving door. To this day, whenever someone complains about some psycho nanny, I always know I can trump them with our tales of woe. It was pure headache for my parents, but now we all relish the retelling. Because you can't make up that shit. And hey, at least they didn't give us shaken baby syndrome. Though they most definitely shook the hell out of my parents.

# 4

# Weird Science
# (Minus Kelly LeBrock)

Some girls love the scent of roses in full bloom, others their mother's perfume. For many, it's rising bread or fresh-baked brownies. But for twisted me, the most intoxicating heaven-sent scent is . . . wait for it . . . gasoline. As a kid I inhaled it while at the pump, causing my mom to freak and roll up the windows for fear of an Exxon-logo-shaped brain tumor on my little noggin. My dad had the same addiction, which we always joked about. I wanted to hook that nozzle up to my nostril and just inhale all day. Bring on the sixty-five-gallon drum so I could do a swan dive into it. Gas stations were my bakeries. Heaven on earth.

In third grade, we began studying the five senses. The most feared teacher in my whole school was my science teacher, Mr. X. Remember Miss Hannigan, who loathes little girls? She's Mother Teresa next to this dude. He walked the halls in his white lab coat and regularly snapped at us, sending shivers up my spine that I still remember.

We dissected frogs at age eight, learning where the Golgi body was versus the spleen. We knew every human organ and bone at nine. Every system in the body by ten. About once every two or three weeks, as we'd all assembled around the lab's black tables, each with our own station, including safety glasses, individual microscopes, dissecting trays, and tools, Mr. X would enter dramatically, like a royal from stage left in a Shakespeare play, grand and with an air of power.

Sometimes he didn't speak but took out four pieces of white paper. Oh shit. We knew what was coming. In silence he would fold the paper and press a hard crease into the stack. Next he'd open it and rip along the line. Gasps. He'd then fold the halves into quarters and crease and rip again. Panting. He would then slowly walk around the room, his shoes clacking on the floor as he passed each girl a small section of paper. Hyperventilation. Pop quiz.

"One. Spell: cytokinesis."

"Two. Spell: *Lumbricus terrestris*."

"Three. Spell: deoxyribonucleic acid."

Shaking, I'd rev up my mechanical pencil (*click click click click!*) taken from my Hello Kitty pencil case, bite my lower lip, and go for it.

After the three terms on our spelling test, he would walk around and collect the small rectangles. In front of the whole class he would announce his findings: "Melanie. Let's see: Yes, no, no. One out of three. Not good." If someone got all of them right, he would give them a curt nod, causing the girl to exhale slowly but not even dare smirk in relief.

If we were doing an experiment, say, peeling back the skin of a *Lumbricus terrestris,* i.e., earthworm, and putting organs under a microscope, and if he felt someone was sloppy or not doing it per his specific instructions, he would walk up slowly, casually take the girl's dissecting tray from her, and dramatically dump the contents in a garbage can.

"Your experiment has been canceled."

Then he would take her three-ring binder, open it,

and dump all the pages into the can on top of the worm guts. Devil.

One day he caught me whispering with my friend and opened the door and asked me to go in the hallway.

*"Get out."*

My heart pounded through my chest like a cartoon getting a boner for the girl skunk or whatever, except instead of cupids in my eyeballs there were skulls. I could feel the stress hormone cortisol coursing through my body as I crossed the lab full of classmates, who looked down at the black lab tables, averting their eyes.

I solemnly did my walk of shame, fighting tears, to the door, which had a bumper sticker that read I [HEART] SCIENCE. Except instead of a heart like on my Hello Kitty pencil case it was an actual heart, like in your chest with tubes and veins and shit. It was organy and he prolly thought it was really clever, but I just thought it was dumb.

Looking back, I swear they could've found twenty heads in his fridge and no one would have been surprised. The stench of formaldehyde from his many jars of fetal pigs and the like still haunts me to this day as the anti-smell, the one I can't abide, the one that makes my skin crawl. But not for the reason you'd think; for most people it would carry the stink of death, but for me it triggers thoughts of Mr. X.

I had this teacher for three years and for that entire period, the two days a week I had science class I woke up with my heart pounding. I loathed him, but he still scared me. Until one day. When I snapped.

I had just had a very disturbing experience unrelated to school. I had been obsessed with *Saturday Night Live* since toddlerhood and so was overjoyed when a friend of the family got a ticket for me. I went to the show and then briefly to the after party, where Don Henley, who had been the musical guest, was holding court. I nervously approached him, the only kid at the party, with the friends of the family who'd scored me the entrée.

"Um, Mr. Henley? Hi, um, I'm Jill. I'm so sorry to interrupt you but I just wanted to say, um, I love your records . . ."

He looked at me with the same glare as Mr. X and responded: "Please. Go. Away."

Yes. To a child. What a fucking douchebag. Like,

beyond. Tears burning their way to my retinas, I was in the cab home within minutes and stormed into my apartment. My parents had waited up to hear all about my night and I ran past them into my room. I kneeled down and took out my Eagles and Don Henley cassette tapes, pulled the wheels to let out some slack, and *yanked* at that thin brown tape with all my might. I pulled and pulled and pulled until all that remained was the empty plastic shell printed with the song titles on each side and a garbled web of tape. Fuck. That. Mother. Fucker. I was enraged. I wish I had said something. I wish I had told him he was a jerk. I wish I had stood up for myself.

A week later, I was back in science class. We had completed the senses of sight, having to label all the parts of a human eye on another quarter-paper pop quiz, as well as sound and taste. Then came the sense of smell. He went around the room and asked each girl to say what her favorite smell was.

"Gardenias!"

"Chocolate-chip cookies!"

"Cinnamon."

Jill's turn:

"Gasoline."

Crickets. The silence was deafening as Mr. X's face warped into a mask of sheer unbridled rage.

"How *dare you* be fresh with me?!" he roared.

I saw the girls in their plaid uniforms around the room straighten in fear for me.

"I'm not," I whispered meekly.

"*Gasoline?!* You can get up and leave my laboratory. Your experiment is *canceled*."

Normally, like any other girl who was cast into the humiliating flames of the hallway, I would have shaken as I gathered my pencil case and notebook and put them in my backpack. But not that day. My young face twisted to match his ire.

"GASOLINE IS MY FAVORITE SMELL! I'M NOT BEING FRESH!" I yelled at his face. "IT HAS ALWAYS BEEN MY FAVORITE SMELL."

"You GET OUT OF MY LABORATORY!" he screamed, his arm shooting toward the door like a Spartan arrow.

"FINE!" I yelled back at him, eyes ablaze, noticing in my peripheral vision the shock of my shivering classmates. "I'M CALLING MY PARENTS AND THEY WILL TELL YOU IT IS MY FAVORITE SMELL!" I stormed out of the lab, slamming the door behind me. On the staircase up to my homeroom, I burst into sobbing convulsive tears. Fuck assholes. Fuck Don Henley. Fuck Mr. X. I opened the door to my floor and ran to the office of Miss Anton—the head of the lower school.

"My goodness, Jill, what is wrong?"

I didn't answer. I reached for her phone, dialed 9 for an outside line, and called home. My mom answered.

"MOM! TELL HER! TELL HER WHAT MY FAVORITE SMELL IS!"

"What?"

"TELL MISS ANTON MY FAVORITE SMELL!"

I handed Miss Anton the phone, chin jutting out and defiant as my mom issued testimony.

"Miss Anton, my daughter's favorite smell is gasoline."

I told Miss Anton that I was kicked out of class because Mr. X refused to believe that my favorite smell was gasoline. Miss Anton walked me back down to the lab. I had wiped away my cataracts of tears and was pink faced but empowered as I burst open the door with squinted eyes.

"Mr. X, a moment?" she said, gesturing to my science teacher. Miss Anton pulled Mr. X aside and whispered as I took my place back at the long black table. The girls looked at me like, *What the hell?* But I sat proud and tall. He listened to her and then glanced at me and then back at her. He thanked Miss Anton for visiting and then apologized to me in front of the class. And guess what? He never messed with me again.

And for that matter, no other guy has. At ten years old, I somehow decided that I was a badass. My skin was thickened and I wouldn't fear bullies. When I bit back, he saw me in a new way and even started writing comments on my perfect quizzes like "good job."

The postscript of this story is twofold. 1) When I left for high school, I later learned Mr. X was shitcanned. He screamed at a trustee's daughter who wept every night before she had science until her father freaked and had him fired. No one knew what happened to him but there was partying in the halls, according to my friends who were at the school after I left. Euphoria. "Ding dong the witch is dead"–style. For years, whenever the gang got together, we'd start to swap stories about his reign o' terror.

2) And then one day, I called my friends *dying*. I made each of them sit down. And I told them the craziest thing. Twenty years after fifth grade, I was walking with my nana Ruth in a mall in South Florida. It was air-conditioned so we decided to walk there instead of outside, with those sliced tennis balls on the bottom of her walker for traction. As we did a lap by the Limited and Victoria's Secret, I noticed two cute fat gay guys in Hawaiian shirts holding hands. One was eating a corn dog on a stick. I love old queens. As we approached, I started to realize, in the sea of chins, that one of them was Mr. X.

"Mr. X?!" I yelled, stopping in my tracks, jaw on floor.

He paused, arm linked with his partner, and looked at me.

"Hello, Jill." He said it the way Jerry Seinfeld addressed Newman.

"You remember me?" I marveled.

"Of course I do."

He said it very calmly, and a small chill just began to make its way up my spine as I recognized that creepsville glint in his eye that I now realized was not unlike Hannibal Lecter's. But then I stopped, realizing without that crisp white lab coat, with an aura of power and the ability to drive me to tears, he was just an ex–science teacher sporting a horrifying floral exploding shirt and was in a mall in West Palm Beach with his old cock-gobbler boyfriend. And it was sad.

"Nice to see you," I said sweetly. "Happy holidays."

I walked away, thinking how strange life is.

PPS: Fuck Don Henley. I met him again later in life, not at a mall, but at a small dinner party, and while I wanted to give him the cold shoulder, I decided to turn on the charm and kill him with kindness. He'd peaked back in the eighties when he was telling little *moi* to scram. How sad to have hit your zenith ages ago. He must be longin' for them good ol' days. Desperado, in fact.

# 5

# Wednesday Addams in Barbietown

I was the vampire of my high school. Okay, I wasn't. But in comparison to the legions of blond fleece-wearing preppies who looked like J.Crew explosions, I might as well have been a tongue-pierced goth. I was pale; I wore black; I never saw a field hockey stick.

Oddly enough, I had begged my parents to let me go away to boarding school. In New York I felt like girls went from twelve right to twenty-one, our teen years sucked out by the social chasm between dumbass charity dances from seven to nine P.M. and then bars. You could either kiss a brace-face boy or dance with older gross men at a club. But where were the "guys"? Like in the John Hughes movies? Not that I wanted to cheer on the football team, or even bite my lower lip Molly-style; I just wanted to be a fucking teenager! So, at fourteen years old, I secretly sent applications to six New England boarding schools. When the time came to get my parents to accompany me to interviews, I sat them down.

"Why would you want to go to boarding school?" my mom asked.

"I went to get away from my parents," my dad added. "Is that what you want?"

I took a deep breath. "You know how last week I said I went to see *Rain Man* and slept at Sara's?"

They nodded.

"Well . . ." I continued with trepidation. "That was a lie. Sara said she was sleeping here and instead of seeing *Rain Man* we went to Mars, a club on the West Side Highway, and danced all night until the sun came up and then we went to a diner in Chelsea and got breakfast and bought the *New York Times* and read the *Rain Man* review so I could discuss it with you."

I was promptly FedExed to boarding school in Connecticut.

When I arrived in my multizipper black leather motorcycle jacket, which I tossed on my bed next to my blond, southern roommate's poster of a fluffy kitten dangling from a branch that said HANG IN THERE!, it was as if I had parked my spaceship on the verdant perfectly mowed quad. It was the first day of school, a crisp gorgeous September day, and old friends were embracing each other as Big Head Todd and the Monsters blared from a "boom box." Except I felt like I was the monster, a bloodsucker descending on this quaint country club of tended grass and blond hair. Whenever it was a big day at school, like mothers' day or fathers' day (separate 'cause of the divorced peeps), graduation, or in this case, the first day of school, they had that square-cut bright green sod patched in what I call toupee grass. Equally sunny-hued were my classmates, unpacking tapestries and bean bag chairs, bedspreads and wardrobes. The clothes were ROYGBIV all the way, ripped from a prism, or a J.Crew catalog, which at the time, 1989, had color choices like Wave, Berry, Lemon, Pumpkin, and Rat Blood. Not really. But they were weird.

And then there was Jill's closet. Black. Brown. Gray. White. Navy was steppin' waaaay out. Going crazy. Boots on my feet instead of Tevas and later black leather clogs instead of Birkenstocks. It was as if Patagonia threw up on the campus; that little mountain logo may as well have been an active volcano that Pompeii'd everyone's ass into fleece for all eternity. Not a soul wandered the halls sans zip-up pile. But it was Indian summer, so Panama Jack was squirted on tan-skinned bikini bods. Hacky Sacks were kicked, Frisbees thrown. Some mop-headed Aryan Nation dudes noodled to the Dead, while others threw lacrosse (aka "lax") balls back 'n' forth.

And then there was me: the angel of death.

I looked exhumed from a grave starting around age eleven when I had a mole removed that had some malignant cells in it. I went promptly under the knife to remove surrounding tissue, got a bunch of stitches and sizable scar, and never went in the sun again. So by high school I was preaching the valor of pallor and was a hue akin to that of Robert Smith of the Cure. *Beetlejuice* had come out and I dug Winona's wan look so I went with it. But I stuck out.

Not as much as I would the second night of school, when we had our first "Vespers." Vespers was a four-times-a-week all-school assembly in the evening, just before dinner, with speakers ranging from political peeps to dance troupes to Bela Fleck and the Flecktones to a gay guy who told all the homophobic male prepsters how hurtful it was when, in his teen years, he was called an anal astronaut.

Everyone was freshly showered after their field hockey practice, a comb run through their baby shampoo–smelling hair, their Laura Ashley–type dresses with cabbage rose infestations tossed on. The guys had to wear jackets and ties, which I loved, and while most of my ensembles were slightly more urban I still liked getting dressed for dinner. But on that night, still a bit shaky from the newness of it all, we had some doctor come lecture us about STDs.

"Everyone, please rise," he commanded. We stood up from our crimson velvet seats.

"If you own a Patagonia jacket, sit down."

Rumbles as 90 percent of the school plopped back in their chairs.

There I stood, looking around at the others—a theater techie here, a singer girl there, a girl from Belgium, and Long Duck Dong.

"Now, if you attended the summer camp Windridge, please sit down."

Uh-oh, there went the singer and even the techie. That left me, some Bangladeshi with Coke-bottle-thick glasses, and Long Duck.

"Okay. Now. Look around you."

I felt sweat gather as the back of my neck reddened with the toast of embarrassment.

"The remaining students standing . . ."

Oh god. What? Don't call me up onstage. Please.

" . . . are representative . . ."

Yeah . . . ?

"Of the number of you that will *die of AIDS*."

Um . . . what?!

Great, I just got here and already I'm dead of AIDS. What a way to become popular! *Finally* he let us sit down as he lectured about the epidemic of HIV and told us that we all had to "bag it up" if we "interdormed." That was code for screwing each other's brains out in boarding school speak and I'd like to add that I never *once* interdormed. Notta once. I had boyfriends from summer camp that I stayed together with, if you count never seeing each other again but writing letters as staying together.

But I could already tell I'd nurse plenty of crushes on all the hot reversible-name types. You know, Brooks Garrett—could be Garrett Brooks! Prescott Burke, Wellington Rutherford, Crawford Hodges. Usually with a roman numeral tacked on the end. It doesn't work with Kopelman Arie, now, does it? Very quickly, however, I learned that said dudes had an annual first-week-of-school tradition where they camped on beach chairs in Main Hall and rated the new girls with cards, grading us. I walked by and the five guys held up cards, old-school Olympics-style, except all the judges may as well've been East German in the early eighties. I think I got a 4.0, which might sound like an A but at my school was a big fat B–, since we had a grading scale that went up to 6.0. Great, just great. It was at this moment I walked straight to the dean of students.

"This is absurd. It's 1989! This is unacceptable!" I ranted. Having come from an all-girls school, I was starting to fear Taft may have been a bad fucking choice. The guys were told to knock it off, but as chairs were being folded and poster board chucked, one guy, whose name was literally Chad, said to me with a chin-jut, "Too bad you're not as hot as your mom."

I guess he'd spied us on move-in day, and yes, my mom is gorgeous, but ouch, was that harsh! But it only empowered me more to forge my own path and make the best of my three years there. I just had to figure out the lay of the land first. A cultural road map. I had to figure out the system, stat.

There were all these rituals I had to learn, not by osmosis but by drowning. Those benches are for seniors only. Touch Abe Lincoln's nose daily for good luck. The freshmen, or "lower-mids," or "lower-squids," were relegated to the balcony in the auditorium. Without fail on movie night, some assholic senior would open the door and scream the ending. (Just as my pulse was pounding as I beheld a squirming Harrison Ford in *Presumed Innocent,* one jock yelled, *"The wife did it!"* and ran out. Thanks.) Lastly, under no circumstances can you drop a tray in the caf, as a symphony of embarrassment and shattered plates would earn you roaring applause from the entire school, five hundred strong.

Some traditions, though, were fabulous. About every three weeks or so after a long night of studying and rumbling late-night tummies, the dorm monitors would run up and down the halls and scream, "FEED! FEED! FEEEEEEED!" When you heard the word "feed" it was like cherubim blaring celestial trumpets, the heavenly siren call of high cuisine: Domino's. Subway. Pillsbury cookie dough logs. Served in the dormitory common room to girls in their pajamas. There were also Headmaster's Holidays, where they'd stage a fake fire drill or assembly and then have someone make an elaborate entrance à la Howard Stern as Fartman on a zip wire to announce that, for no reason other than to just be cool, there would be no school the next day. Amazing.

What was not amazing was being in what I called the Two-Jew Club in my class of 180. Though in addition there was a halfsie girl whose was "accused" of being a heeb by one of the white-baseball-hat people and she violently responded, *I AM NOT JEWISH!* recoiling as if he'd asked her if she liked to snack on snake feces. "My mother is Scandinavian!" Blithely eating my chocolate pudding, I responded casually, "Newsflash: with a last name like yours, you'd be rounded up with the rest of us, honey."

Despite the homogeneous student body at Taft, I met two of my best friends there, Lisa and Lauren, who remain sisters to this day. We were three brunettes in the sea of *Children of the Corn* towheads, and while the fleecefest boasted bootlegged Phish and Grateful Dead, we'd blare Sub Pop records from my room and talk about who'd lose their virginity when. Mine was like a burden. Like not having your period in *Are You There God? It's Me, Margaret*. In both cases, I wanted blood. Call me a vaginal vampire, but I wanted to be old. Der. Older. I wanted to be edgy, provocative, on the dark side, like when a ween entered you, you somehow had your passport stamped (or punched is more like it) and you crossed over into some new land of the deflowered, seeing the world through new eyes. And speaking of foreign travel, due to alleged blood-letting post–hymen plunder, the three of us started referring to losing our V card as "going to Japan." Picture the flag. Yup: white with a big fucking red dot. We learned in history class that in medieval villages after the wedding night they'd hang up the sheet to show the whole town that the new couple had consummated the marriage. I mean . . . *ew*! Yet in my own way I wanted to verbally wave the sheet by staying up all night and dishing about it with my friends when it happened. As it did after junior year, in a very anticlimactic romp, with "Ouch!" instead of the "Oh god" I'd seen in movies. Oh well. By senior year I wanted to pole-vault the hell out into college and move on with my life—and the sweet smiles and photos with ten girls in a row with their arms around one another in floral dresses save for *moi,* Elvira (my friends and parents would always sing that *Sesame Street* song, "One of these things is not like the others!"), started to feel staged and desperate in their attempts to capture the Best Years of Our Lives. I remember one preppy seersucker-sportin' alumnus dad patting his daughter on the back, saying, "Kids, enjoy it; these are the best years of your life!" Note to self: buy rope for noose at school store. In the end, it wasn't the horror show some paint of high school, nor was it the John Hughesian all-American pigskin paradise with slamming lockers and Psychedelic Furs as soundtrack. It was . . . fine. And some moments were downright fun, if not a tad weird. We got so wound up we were drawn to random pranks at all hours. Lore had it the seniors a few years above me broke into the science lab and chucked thirty fetal pigs off the balcony during Movie Night while squealing. They stole statues from rival Hotchkiss (boo, hiss!), somehow drove the headmaster's car into the lobby, or covered the small pond with floating red lunch trays. Our pranks were far less of a spectacle but my senior year we did streak (my one and only time—some lucky frosh was brushing his teeth and unleashed a soprano "Holy shit!"). My most memorable bizarre stunt was fall of senior year as we were all dying of stress. This girl in the dorm decorated her door for each month, and after Halloween's bats 'n' jackos came November's turkey in a top hat and a horn of plenty that put the "corn" in "cornucopia." Literally. She had three Indian corncobs tied with a bow made out of corn husk. At about three A.M., feeling completely bonkers, Lauren and I ripped it off her door and stuck it in the microwave. We were shocked and delighted to see that it popped. We replaced the popped cobs on the door as if nothing had happened. Hand to god, the next morning she marveled at it, saying, "*Whoa, guys!* It must've been really hot in the hallway!" No shit.

And being locked into a dorm room at ten forced me

to make friendships that remain some of the closest in my life; you bond on a whole different level (or despise on a whole new one, too, in some cases) when you're trapped with each other. And so for that I'm glad. Two great friends made it all worth it. And to this day, when I sic myself on a buffet, sumo-style, one blissful word pops up, wired in pink neon in the storefront of my mind: "FEED!"

# 6

# Tea with Dracula

I have a weird relationship with tampons. You know how most girls have euphemisms for periods? You know, like, "on the rag," "Aunt Flo is in town," "checking into the Red Roof Inn," "the Communists are invading the summer house," etc.? Well, I actually have that with 'pons. I call them vampire tea bags. Or cunt plugs. Just kidding, I never called them that. I'm so grossed out by them, and yet, really, what am I gonna do, lie in my hut for a week a month like a pygmy? As a virgin at thirteen when I first got my crimson tide, it didn't even cross my mind to ride the cotton pony. I'd simply use a pad. Which, might I add, as a 1974 baby, did *not* include a belt. When I cracked *Are You There God? It's Me, Margaret* and I read about their pads with belts, I was like, *What the fuck are they talking about?!* When my own Cracky Chan enlisted in the red army during intermission at *Forbidden Broadway,* my mom smiled and kvelled and misted, then took my hand and brought me to a twenty-four-hour drugstore, and those weren't as omni back in the eighties. We bought my adhesive pads and that was that. Womanhood was so close I could smell it. Literally. Ew, that was gross, sorry. Anyway, at first, everyone used pads. I barely even knew what a tampon was!

Actually, that's not true.

My mom had a stash of Tampax in a basket thing to the right of her toilet, which seemed quite mysterious when I was a little kid of, say, seven or eight. On the other side was a magazine rack with *Vogue* and *People.* Weird combo, I know, but she insists today that *People* was a comped subscription from my dad's work. I remember one cover was Ann Jillian with her platinum bangs/bowl cut and she'd had breast cancer and said something like "I hope I'm not any less a woman for my husband" or something like that and I was so young I didn't even know what that meant. Also unclear? What those paper-wrapped cigar things were in the teal box.

Years later, of course, Bill Clinton actually did insert a cigar into a vag, but my kid self wondered what the hell they were and for some reason I don't recall ever asking. But little by little my mom's tampons would disappear. She was always buying and opening new boxes.

Then one day, my mom was cleaning my brother's room and reached under his bed. I heard a scream. I came running from my room to find my mom lying on his green carpet, peering under his bed, jaw on the floor. "*Willieeeeeee!*" she yelled.

I got down on my hands and knees and was shocked to find *hundreds* of tampons piled under the box spring. My four-year-old brother came scampering down the hall-way in his Velcro sneakers.

"Yeah?" he asked in the doorway, finding us on the floor.

"Willie, what is this?" she asked him, revealing his compromised stash and her handful of cardboard plungers with strings coming out.

"Oh." He shrugged. "That's my dynamite."

It was the definition of "LOL." It totally did look like TNT, shipped direct from Acme Products, sold by one

Wile E. Coyote for my mother's 'ginee. Nice one, Will.

So tamps were sealed into family lore, and it was soon revealed what they were for and I was horrified. When my own flag of Japan waved in the teenage breeze, I was a pad gal through 'n' through. And then peer pressure hit me. Not for brewskis or BJs, but for cooter corks. Little by little all my friends started pooning up. Every Shark Week, I tried, but it killed. I was closed for bidniss down there, nailed shut, sealed up.

"But don't you hate messy pads?" both commercials and my friends asked.

"Uh, yeah . . ."

"So just try it!"

I did. Again and again and again. And I felt like I was being raped by Raggedy Andy's cotton cock. I would stab my seemingly sewn-shut vag with the applicator till I'd give up, thinking it hurt so much, and it was a slender regular; what the eff would I one day do when a big ol' ween tried to enter? Maybe mine was like those tunnels that didn't have height clearance for certain-sized vehicles. Like the SUV of penii couldn't even get into there.

But then one day I had an incident. I was wearing a skirt and was walking home at the brisk pace most New Yorkers whizz by with. And before I could even do a damn thing about it, my bloody maxi pad somehow became unglued from my panties and fell through my panty leg hole *sunny-side up* onto Madison Avenue. Right there in front of Fred Leighton on Madison and Sixty-sixth Street. Diamonds, emeralds, sapphires, and rubies sparkled in the glittering window and my own ruby mess lay on the sidewalk. So I did what any mortified, ashamed girl would do. *RUN, FORREST, RUN!*

Shortly thereafter, I got to boarding school, and a

senior, aghast that I actually walked around with a white pillow in my Calvins, took me by the wrist and led me to the bathroom. "I'm going to talk you through this, through the stall door," she announced.

"I'm ready," I said, exhaling, bracing myself.

"Okay," she said, "now, the way you were describing the discomfort, I feel like you were trying to shoot it up—"

"Uh, well, yeah . . . isn't that how it goes?"

"No!" she exclaimed. "No, no. The hole doesn't go up, it's diagonal. Don't aim parallel to your belly button, aim toward your butt crack."

"Huh?"

"Angle it toward your ass."

I tilted the cotton rocket.

And then, *blast off*!

*Eureka!*

Halle-fucking-lujah.

The gun was loaded.

# 7

# I Am a Gay Man Trapped in a Woman's Body

After three years of ribbon-belt 'splosion, I was all excited for my new chapter at multiculti college. When I said I was going to Yale, countless morons immediately reminded me that they "heard New Haven is really dangerous," and that "one out of four, maybe more" members of the student body was homosexual. Which wasn't enough for me! That's because I have always truly felt that I am a gay man.

It's not like "Oh, all my friends are gay guys." Well, yes, that too, but I also weirdly think I am a queen. As in, I know every Tim Rice lyric ever penned. I've never missed a Tonys. I don't know who Patti LuPone is from that oh-blah-dee oh-blah-da Down syndrome TV show; I worship her from the Great White Way. Nary a car ride isn't blaring Andrew Lloyd Webber. When I was seven, my mother and I went to the box office for *Evita* tickets. My little head peeked up to the ticket window, requesting a pair of matinee seats, orchestra.

"Um, ma'am, I'm not sure this is appropriate for her," the cashier said, gesturing to me.

"Oh, she's already seen it four times," my mother replied, sliding the credit card through the hole.

I can perform a one-woman version of most Broadway shows. But it's not just 'cause of an affinity for original cast recordings that I'm a poof. I'm drawn to gay men. I love their style. Okay, maybe not the bear scene at Rawhide on lower Eighth *avec* full chauffeur hat and leather vest over flesh. But in general: they are gorgeous! And tasteful. And interesting. We like the same things.

Dick, for one. Just kidding. Slash not. I love me a diva. Before I bore fruit, I clubbed at the Cock and dance-halled my way into some serious street cred, and even had a glam rock–themed birthday party with my best friend Trip called Studio Filthy Whore. It was maje. The invitation read "No Glitter, No Entry." And BTW, if I were a real pink-triangle card-carrying fag, I wouldn't be just some mere hipster with a Strokes haircut and John Varvatos 'splosion. No. I'd be Johnny Weir times ten, faaaabulous and *en fuego,* a foot off the ground like a homo hovercraft, floating higher than a combination triple axel double sal-chow. I'd sweat sparkles and diarrhea sequins. My drag name would be Helvetica Bold. (Alas, years after I decided this, I heard that was taken. Damn.) I've read countless books about coming out and am a member of Lambda. My interest in the early days of AIDS, when it was called GRIDS (gay-related immune deficiency syndrome), bor-dered on obsession, especially the fact that it was ignored for so long. (No doubt if it'd been little white babies get-ting Kaposi's sarcoma there would have been a five-alarm deafening insta-war on the virus.) And before the national debate began I was fixated on the injustice of gays' inabil-ity to marry.

But for all of my righteous rainbow flaggage there was one glaring hole (no pun intended): oddly, I never had one lesbo pal. Not by choice or anything; I just didn't know any. So when I got to college and saw a group called Yales-bians, and subsequently an even more hard-core group, a Jewish faction of extreme religious box-chowers called

OrthoDykes, I was surprised at my bizarrely unexplainable semihomophobia. It wasn't a phobia per se—I wasn't freaked or anything—it was more that I just . . . didn't identify. Lady Gaga? *Bien sûr!* Indigo Girls? No, *gracias*. From the mullets to the shoe-boots, I couldn't aesthetically absorb the culture the way I did with my boys, even though I wanted to. And I'm *such* a girl's girl! And truly, it's not that I'm freaked about carpet munchage (which, okay, maybe I am, I'll admit), it's more the look and feel. When I go to my favorite bar in New York, Marie's Crisis, on Grove Street, I feel more at home among the singing gay guys than I would in a bar full of ladies at Henrietta Hudson or Rubyfruit (which is code for clit, I think). One night, I was early for a dinner on the Lower East Side. I spied Meow Mix, the lez bar, and decided I was intrigued and would get a drink there. I just wanted to spy the scene. Was it going to be the PowerLez clique like on *Sex and the City*? Lipstick wearers with stilettos? I was curious.

Apparently, so was Michael Imperioli, best known as "Christophuh" on *The Sopranos*. He walked in and sat on the stool next to me, looking me over, assuming that I was a muff diver. We made small talk about the weather and the music, chatting in the end for about a half an hour. The funny thing is I never could have struck up a conversation anywhere else, because he prolly would have assumed I was some stalkerazzi fame-fucker who would try to bang the eyebrows off him and Glenn Close some rabbits on his stove. But no, I was a nice downtown hip lesbian; how unthreatening! When I left he said it was so nice talking to me and rubbed my arm good-bye as I sauntered out, presumably for my dinner with k.d. lang.

My eldest child, who has gay godparents, blithely checks out the wedding announcements in the *New York Times* and asks me to read stories of how the pairs met. She has no idea that in (many) parts of the country—not to mention the world—the marriages are not legal. She sees two people in love. I'm not some kind of beaming psychomom whose sense of accomplishment is tied up in her chitlins, but I must confess I'm so proud my kids are color-blind and little unknowing rainbow-flag wavers. Moms are aghast when I say I'll be fine if my son, Fletch, lives on Christopher Street and skips to work, but it's the truth. Then I'll always have a pal around the corner when I want a midnight croon session at Marie's Crisis. Anyone who goes there, even people who are dragged in rolling their eyes, can't help but feel a jolt of camaraderie and New York spirit gathered around the packed piano with perma, 365-days-a-year Christmas lights. Between the tiny twinkling bulbs and the improvised four-part harmonies, I feel more alive than I feel in any other place in the city. "I could have daaaaaanced all night" rings out as people cram under the wooden beams, singing and swaying. I feel merry and warm and part of a club. I feel gay. I know the art clique leader that Charlotte befriended on *Sex and the City* said, "If you don't eat pussy, you're not a dyke," but I still feel that connection. More to the guys, but still. Maybe it's an outsider thing. Maybe I just dig the same stuff. Maybe I see the world in the same way. Through a kaleidoscope, where the poppies are redder, Emerald City is greener, and Judy Garland's voice is more magical than Oz.

## 8

# Everybody's Gotta Start Somewhere

I know, I know: I'm not the first gal who *detested* her boss and had nightmares for years about fetching coffee with just the right ratio of skim milk to java. But I am one of the proud few who've had a tape dispenser thrown at her head. No, people, not the clear plastic Scotch roll; I'm talking the office-supply-style, weighted, pull-'n'-rip desktop kind. During college, I'd had internships at *Harper's Bazaar* and MTV and the now defunct *Mademoiselle* magazine, where I actually worked for Kate Spade, who was the nicest person I'd ever met, let alone worked for, so the bar had been raised pretty fucking high. Then came Richard Sinnott, accessories director at *Bazaar* under Liz Tilberis, who is a comic genius. Richard and I cackled the hours away, hit gay bars, and even experimented with online shenanigans when the Internet started. Holy shit, that makes me sound super old. "Back in ye olde days, before there was any Internet . . ."

Anyway, I was twenty-one and my first job out of college was as an assistant at a pop culture magazine; I'd be allowed to write certain blurbs and "front of book" articles now and again. At first it seemed like a dream job; in fact I was reminded by the head of HR that "thousands of kids would kill for this job" and that $18,000 was "really generous" considering that "quite frankly, people would pay us to work here."

Lies. Give 'em a week and they'd have jumped out the fucking window. Did I mention there was no lunch hour? Oh no, that was too postal workery. "We all work through lunch and maybe take a ten-minute break," I was told. So, wait, like, no hour to myself to get an eyebrow wax and proper meal? "This is a magazine. We could fill your job with any number of people who would *kill* to work through lunch." The result was ten pounds gained. I'd starve all day and then get out at ten at night and sic myself on a *huge* dinner. Which I subsequently learned was how the Japanese make sumo wrestlers so fucking fat.

They fast and then pound a massive buffet and crash, all those calories on their asses and in donut rolls. Great. That would be me. Without the black flappy diaper thing, but still. Not good. I had one friend, in another department, who was equally miserable, but the others around me were all my superiors.

Technically, I had three bosses. One woman, two guys. The woman would routinely call people retards and storm in enveloped in a beige cloud of cigarette smoke and farts. I went to work with my heart pounding every day. After only a few weeks, I started to cry in the bathroom. This was a soul-draining experience that went on for twenty months, generally in the afternoons after a verbal beating.

It all began with the cheese Danish. But not just any cheese Danish—the almighty, the mack daddy, the pooh-bah, the grandmommy of all cheese danii: a Danish from Dean & Deluca on Prince Street. Each morning I was sent to fetch Her Majesty a cheese Danish. And one at lunch. And one at four or five P.M. I swear, people, if she collapsed and dropped dead and the autopsy people sliced her open, cheese Danish stuffing would just ooze out. Too gross. Add two packs of cigarettes a day, nine espressos, and lack of hygiene, and you've got what I call B cubed: bad breath, bad BO, bad box.

Now, you know that the shit's bad when I tell you that she wasn't even the worst one. Her beeyotch butt boy looked like a Gaston-esque caricature of a ripped Chelsea queen, black turtleneck and black Helmut Lang pants daily, like *Sprockets* but without the Nazi accent. But make no mistake: he ran the joint Gestapo-style. There was a strict no-food policy. I wasn't exactly sure why, until our gorgeous loft space had a visitor. From the order Rodentia. A small rat darted down the long hallway and I levitated onto my desk *screaming*. No doubt the critter was lured by the aroma of fresh-baked piping-hot cheese Danish, and he strutted down the gray carpet by my desk. Chaos ensued. Shrieks were heard around the office and a photo editor dropped a pile of folders and bolted, papering the floor with outtakes of Bruce Weber shot next to half-naked boys with water spritzed on their chests.

Exterminators were called and that was the end of *Ratatouille*. It was around this time that, realizing my thigh circumference was approaching hula hoop girth, I decided I needed to start sneaking in a healthy small lunch or snack. I couldn't slave for twelve hours working up the appetite of a T. rex and then stuff face *avec* two bread baskets before the apps were even served.

I had a bag of baby carrots in my top drawer, next to the paper clips and stapler. When no one was looking, I'd crunch one with super-slow chews and silently swallow. This worked for a few weeks. Then one day, holding a telltale carrot stump, I was caught red-handed. Or I guess orange-handed.

My boss's shadow loomed over me. When I looked up, his face was contorted as if the rage boiling inside him would blast through his nostrils, ears, and eye sockets, sending his eyeballs flying all around the room like those bright rubber ones in the twenty-five-cent supermarket dispensers. He then walked off.

Later in the day, I went to pee and came back to my desk to find a note. It was an eight-and-a-half-by-eleven-inch piece of standard white paper crisply folded in half with a crease that was obviously pressed with some sort of object like a CD case or a knife handle. It was then stapled around the entire border, with the little silver staples making a thin metal line around the three sides.

I pried open the Fort Knox memo and found the following.

*Jill:*

*It was very curious to see you eating food at your desk. Especially because when we had the rodent problem, you were the one who screamed the loudest. How interesting, then, that you choose to eat in the office . . .*

*B.*

I mean . . . *insane*! Yeah, I'm so sure it was *my* fault. Gee, I'm just certain it had *nothing whatsoever* to do with the *CHEESE DANISH CRUMBS ALL OVER THE FUCKING FLOOR.*

A couple months later, I was fact-checking a David Bowie article and found an error on the final final pass at the eleventh hour. Seriously, it was eleven P.M. and we were all exhausted and wanted to ship the damn issue. I went into a senior staff meeting and said we had to make a last-minute change, which meant we'd be late to newsstand. My boss picked up her tape dispenser and threw it. At me. It hit my head, and while I had a

Snoopy moment where I thought I saw flying Wood-stocks tweeting in a circle around my wounded noggin, I was fine. No lawsuits, though I probably could have sued for any number of things, including mental torture.

I decided I needed to pick a date. A distant magical endpoint, a dot of light far away I could reach out toward and use to pull myself through the muck, like Andy Dufresne escaping Shawshank through a river of doody, but it's worth it to get to the rain and crane shot on the other side. I needed to figure out what my three foot-ball fields would be—another year? No, fuck no. Nine months? Okay, nine months.

Christmas was approaching and the whole office was invited out to a sit-down holiday lunch. We arrived at a nearby restaurant to find that the editor and publisher were only "stopping by" for a total of fifteen minutes—they didn't drink or eat and bolted when we had our appe-tizers cleared. When we came back to our desks each of us had a red rectangular envelope stuck into our keyboards with gold script that read: "Thank You!"

In between the "thank" and the "you" was an oval. In the oval was Benjamin Franklin's face. Wait . . . WTF? Was this . . . a doorman's envelope? It was.

"What the hell is this?" I said, opening it to find a $100 bill.

"Oh, it's our tip. It's not really enough to be a bonus," replied my coworker, whose name was Jil but with one *l*.

She looked at my blank face.

"Yeah, I know, weak." She shrugged. "We can go buy ourselves a sweater at Banana Republic."

I decided nine months would become six. Six months I could do. I gave my notice on my birthday and never looked back. I was free! I was leaving for a job as a copywriter at Bertelsmann Music Group and couldn't have been happier to bail. I think I left Road Runner skid marks on the way out.

When I got to my gleaming new offices and nice boss, I was in shock. At 4:59 P.M. everyone's coats were on and the elevators were jammed with a mass exodus. My second day, I hovered in my boss's door.

"Um, h-hi," I stammered after he'd hung up his phone. "Um, I wanted to see if I could um quickly pop out for a few minutes to grab something to eat?"

He looked at me like I had just parked my spaceship in Times Square. "Why don't you take your lunch hour?"

I looked at him in a daze . . . hour . . . Hour? *Hour!* I had a lunch hour! Yee-*haw*! I was in heaven. No matter what I had to endure—including one schmuck who always had me redo things when he'd originally said he wanted the opposite (and also he wore a bolo tie; not sure which was worse)—I always knew I had an hour that was mine to recharge my batteries. In the end, though, it turned out that office life was not for *moi*. I bailed for the greener pastures of writing solo, and while lonely sometimes, it's sure better than fetching cheese Danishes and being called retarded. Life's just too damn short.

# 9

Obsessed / Detest

## OBSESSED

Dannon coffee yogurt

Woody Allen movies

Nine Inch Nails

Edward Gorey books

Tim Burton's drawings

The sound of billiard balls clacking

The half-opened popcorn kernels at the bottom of
    the bucket

Fat toddler feet

Stories from doctor friends about nasty-ass ER people
    (à la the four-hundred-pound woman who had
    half a tuna sandwich in one of her fat folds, et al.)
    and teratomas (Google it, if you dare)

Nerds

Baked goods

Machine hot chocolate

Texting

Trendy Japanese kids

## DETEST

Thumb rings

Ventriloquists

People posting pix of themselves on private jets on
Facebook

canada

People who have made-up, trying-to-be-cool titles on
their start-up business cards, like "Dreamer-in-
Chief" or "Head Ninja"

Images of animals in human clothing

Morphing babies so they can talk in movies and
    commercials

Toe rings

Ventriloquists' dummies

The Eagles (see Don Henley = asshole anecdote on
    page 41)

Cirque du So Lame

Crocs on grown-ups who aren't surgeons

Hard-candy plastic being unwrapped during a show
    or movie

(sk)Anklets smashed under nude hose (double
    whammy)

Loud gum chewers

People who use "summer" as a verb

# 10

# A Letter to My Crappy
# One - Bedroom

Dearest Apartment No. 5,

Some girls chart the chapters of their lives by jobs or guys or haircuts; I do it by real estate. You, no. 5, are inextricably linked to every memory I have from the mostly heinous fucking four years we spent together, but in the end, you were the one that built me back up from lonely twenty-four-year-old whimpering kvetch subsumed with worries about the Future. I arrived scarred and feeble and left you happy, relieved, and not roping up a noose. But we both know it wasn't easy.

When we met, I was as maudlin as tattered Cosette in the Les Miz poster. I may as well've had a mop and actual shredded clothes, I was so down. Or, as Kit De

*Luca, the whore best friend in* Pretty Woman, *said, "Cinderfuckinrella." I hoped in a new space I could turn my life around. You were way more charming than the other shitboxes I'd seen on my Tasmanian Devil whirlwind tour of way-too-expensive hovels that looked like Czech rat holes you'd crawl in to die. Your exposed brick and dreamy location near Central Park didn't soothe my weary bones and battered emotions, though. That would take some time.*

*The hot Israeli movers came to pack me up from my downtown abode, which was a hipster gigantor luminous loft compared to you, my dark third-floor walk-up. Let's admit it, my sweet, you were definitely a downgrade. The movers found me tearstained and sitting on a cardboard box, refugee-style.*

*"Breakup move?" one asked with a sympathetic look.*

*Whoa. ESP? "Mm-hmm," I sniffled, wiping a hot errant tear.*

*"Don't worry, honey, we do this all the time. You're gonna be just fine."*

*When I was fully moved in, my sitcom-style reverie of hot-neighbor sexual tension was dashed instantly: of the ten apartments, eight were occupied by single women.*

*Grrrreat. Of the remaining two tenants, one was a family with three kids and the other lived behind a buzzer reading "Erlichman." I held out hope for an NJB (Nice Jewish Boy), but he turned out to be an AARP-card carrier who told me his rent control had him paying $300 a month, compared to my nightmarish monthly ka-ching that was more than six times that.*

*"The landlord would love to see me go, but I got news for him," he told me in the stairwell, which was adorned with horrifying pheasant-covered wallpaper. "They'll be taking me outta here in my coffin."*

*Good times!*

*Then the gal directly upstairs moved out (got married, migrated to the 'burbs) and in came cocaine-snorting, Moby-blaring Melanie, the town bicycle—and I mean every guy in New York had a ride. I didn't know which was worse—the song "Bodyrock" playing on a loop, like seriously*

*eleventy times in a row, or the bumping of her iron bed from the dick du jour pounding her.*

*Meanwhile, for normal non-druggie* moi, *there was* pas d'*action for a while. While I loved being out of a high-rise and into your intimate, cozier perch, the views of hand-holding couples squoze lemon juice on the wound of my singledom. The nights with you were very lonely sitting on an explosion of Pottery Barn, stuck with racing thoughts that stomped on top of each other, collage-like, inside my head. Would I die in this apartment alone? Like the dude upstairs, would they carry my lifeless bod down the walk-up steps?*

*If being alone with my thoughts got to be too unbearable, I would turn on my el cheapo crappy TV that was so small I might as well have been watching the rich yuppie across the street's giant plasma flat-screen. That's when I learned that four* A.M. *is the loneliest hour. Why do they show so many upsetting movies in the middle of the night? I remember watching* Jagged Edge *and* Single White Female *alone, and somewhere around the time Jennifer Jason Leigh jams her stiletto through the guy's eyeball socket into his brain and kills him, I thought to myself,* This might not be the best thing to watch all alone in the middle of the night. *I think deep down I wanted to take the plunge into my despair over my breakup and really feel the pain. And I did. I woke up with what Humbert Humbert called* pavor nocturnus—*complete and total, all-enveloping night panic. You know, heart pounding for no reason, cold sweats, racing brain, thoughts of spinsterhood.*

*There were two things that calmed me down: infomercials and my best friend, Vanessa. From midnight Chinese food Hoover-vac feasts to psycho long walks to endless phonefests into the wee hours, Vanessa was like the sister-slash-shrink I never had. I once saw a needlepoint pillow that said, "True friends are the ones you can call at 3:00 A.M.," and we all know needlepoint pillows don't lie. During my loneliest, saddest hours of drop-the-toaster-oven-in-my-bubble-bath despair, I would dial her. I'd cry to her that I wished I could have a time machine, Michael J. Fox–style (minus the being-broken-and-needing-weapons-grade-plutonium part), so I could go back and be with my ex. I missed him, us, our life as a team.*

*Vanessa told me sternly that it was time to date—a guy wasn't going to fly through my window while I was watching*

Law & Order *marathons. I had to take control of my life and not whimper. And so began the dates from Hades.*

*There was one blind date who looked not unlike Danny DeVito. Buh-bye. Another had hands that were all palm— you know, huge palms the size of a slice of Wonder Bread, with short, stubby fingers like five pigs in blankets glued onto the Wonder Bread slice. Then there was a cute but way-too-snobby writer who snapped at me that my fidgeting with the Equal packets on the table was "really aggravating." Another guy "would never set foot in Europe."*

*Then, finally, a dream date with a sexy hipster rock critic—we laughed all night in a little café in the pre-chic Lower East Side and he said he'd had the best time and wanted to hang out the next evening. And then when I said I had tickets to a Billy Joel concert, he asked me if I was joking. And I said no, and then a mysterious headache came on and he said he had to go and I never heard from him again.*

*Then, about a year later, after a couple of failed mini-relationships, I really hit the nadir. For some reason all my best friends had boyfriends and I bitterly lamented the fact that I was utterly and completely alone. Except I wasn't. I had roommates. Small, furry gray roommates.*

*The shrieks began when a* pavor nocturnus *fit woke me. Then I had that inner battle of do I deal with getting out of bed to pee or not? I tried go back to sleep but once I recognized my bladder, I had to eventually go. I was heading to the bathroom when I first saw a mouse. It darted across your two-by-two-foot kitchenette and I thought I was going to pass out. I tripped and fell, scraping my knee on the Pottery Barn sisal, not caring about the blood gushing out of my knee as much as the fact that I was living among Rodentia.*

*I called your owner and freaked. Her cold response? "Welcome to New York, kid." I informed her I was from New York and never had four-legged squatters. She dispatched her exterminating company, Roachbusters, whose logo naturally was the Ghostbusters sign with a cockroach instead of Casper. Nice. Two weeks later, I could hear them still scampering. I called your owner again, saying perhaps if she had sent a company called Mousebusters, we wouldn't have this problem. Eventually, thanks to mousetraps, which I had the pleasure of hearing snap in the night, the problem was solved.*

*But the mice forced me, more than anything else, to*

*make plans for every single night. Gone were the dates with Orville Redenbacher and Time Warner cable—I had to leave to avoid other sightings. I literally made a voiced-out-loud pact with the mice that they could hang as long as I never saw or heard them and they shat under the sink.*

*So I started leaving you and going out. All the fucking time. If I didn't have plans, I'd put on my earphones and just take crazy walks, I mean for miles and miles, à la Forrest Gump, minus the beard and retardation. And I started going to plays again, even by myself. One theatrical plunge was so therapeutic it began to take over my life. You must have wanted to shoot me for blaring* Hedwig and the Angry Inch *every second for a year. My friend Trip and I went to see the amazing musical in the West Village, and when we came out, I was singing the songs at the top of my lungs down Jane Street. He stopped and looked in my eyes.*

*"You're back," he said, putting his hands on my shoulders. "We lost you there for a little while, but now you're back."*

*I burst into happy tears because deep down, I knew he was right. I hadn't been fully myself in my previous relationship and I was finally returning to my kooky uncensored side, saying once-bleeped things like "cunt" or "cock gobbler."*

*Then, as winter thawed, I continued to leave you; those long walks I was taking became longer walks—to Wall Street and back to Seventy-sixth, even round-trips to Brooklyn. So I thought I'd walk the New York City Marathon; why the hell not get a medal for this shit? So I did. Seeing as how I am the worst athlete ever to roam this earth (think JV volleyball benchwarmer), it was a true miracle that I finished it. I think it was some crazy challenge for myself and I knew I'd never do it again, but I had to do it once just to prove after nights and nights of lonely walks that I could actually leave you and go into the world. All five boroughs, to be exact.*

*My cute parents were freezing at the finish line, waiting for me complete with GO, JILL, GO! signage, not realizing I'd finished way earlier than planned, so I staggered home alone in my silver cape thingy and, of course, my ribboned medal. I remember walking in and looking around your space. I was exhausted and could barely haul myself to the shower, but I felt so proud because, despite the fact that my body was near collapse, my head was strong.*

*A few months later, I was offered a blind date with a*

guy named Harry my grandma Ruth fixed me up with—he was the grandson of her friend Betty. My first thought was one word: Oy. And then: Not again. I had already been set up by my grandmother with another pal's grandson, who showed up to our date with his boyfriend.

"I'm totally gay and my grandmother would drop dead if she knew," he said apologetically, noticing I'd clearly spent all afternoon getting a mani-pedi and blowout. "But we'll have a great dinner anyway." And we did. But still. Another Nana fix-up?

After relaying this story to Betty, she assured me, "My Harry is straight!" Just what I needed, a dweeb who is such a power nerd he needs his nana for a fix-up with an NJG. But my life was so shtetl, because sure enough it was practically love at first sight for me. He was a beyond-adorable, scruffy nugget in his Harvard ski team pants (double whammy hotness factor of brains and balls), and after dinner we walked and talked and venue-hopped for hours. Finally at four A.M. he put me in a cab and gave me a kiss on the cheek, asking if we could have dinner again two nights later. Natch I said yes, beaming and giddy.

Unlike many nights coming home to you, I was elated.

*There had been so many evenings of dashed hopes after a supposedly fun party where I was in the back of the cab, hanging it up for the night, my only fun to be with* Saturday Night Live *upon my return.*

*But this time, as I put my key in your door, I heard the phone ringing. Huh? I ran up the stairs and saw the clock reading 4:17 as I picked up. "I just wanted to make sure you got home safe," Harry said.*

*The next morning at my* Sex and the City–*style recon brunch with Vanessa, I told her I'd met my husband. And it turned out I was right. Twenty months later we were married and it was your threshold he carried me over when we returned from our honeymoon. Being in love made your ceiling's peeling paint less of an eyesore, the cacophony of the tenants more muted, and the gray critters less scary. Suddenly you were a palace—well, maybe not quite a palace, but my rose-tinted glasses certainly transformed you from lonely bachelorette pad to love nest, filled with the smells of cooking for two instead of microwave-popcorn-as-dinner in sweatpants.*

*Apartment no. 5, sometimes I think if only I'd had a crystal ball, I would have enjoyed our time together much more. If I had known I'd fall in love and be settled with work and be happy, I could have relished those years and not stressed so much. But then I realize, knowing the future would have fucked it up, because it was my hard times with you that got me to where I needed to be. It was in the four walls of your living room that I pep-talked myself back from the Debbie Downer days. It was in your bedroom that I chatted with my best friends. Sure, I was lonely, but that time alone helped solidify not only what I wanted but also who I really was. In the end, the fairy-tale ending was not because of Harry; he didn't save me—you did. You helped me get independent; you returned me to my old self and delivered me to Harry when I was ready. And that is why, despite my nightmare neighbors and cheesy pheasant hallway wallpaper and mice, I am so happy we met. I don't miss you, but I will always love you.*

# 11

# My Vagina Is the Holland Tunnel

CANKLES

It was almost as if the moment I peed on the stick I got fat. Like literally as the plus sign appeared, my ass hit the plus-sized rack. I started to sense the telltale symptoms (tingling boobies, bitchiness) and went to Zitomer's to buy the test. Holy fucking shit. I had to spread 'em and give birth. It was nine months away, *but still*. How to tell Harry? I was going to wrap the little urine-y wand in a box with tissue paper and tell my husband that way, but then it occurred to me that maybe it was too gross to hand him my waste products. We have this thing where we never *ever* have taken a dump with the door open. If someone starts to drop trou and hit the pot, one of us will yell "*Romance!*" (as in, let's at least try to keep the romance alive) as a signal for the other to please shut the door. I remember that *Sex and the City* episode where Miranda's one-night stand takes a fierce dookie, sending her cat sprinting out of the bathroom, Usain Bolt–style, with a tortured "RRRRREAR!" no doubt from the brown cloud he was just enveloped in.

So ixnay on the eestickpay. Instead, I walked next door to Zitomer's (cue finger quotes) "Department Store," i.e., glorified pharmacy. The same place I'd just bought the preggo test, incidentally. In their "department" for kids they had some little socks with lions on them, which were perfect since I call my husband LC, short for Lion Cub, because he in fact resembles a lion with his mane o' locks. Don't worry, he's not, like, in Metallica; he just has a full head of curly brown hair.

I called his cell to see when he'd come out of the train so I could run and meet him on the street—I couldn't even wait the extra few minutes for him to get home. He unwrapped the teeny socks and his jaw dropped. We hugged and promptly celebrated by hitting an Italian restaurant, where I might as well have duct-taped the plate of gnocchi to my thighs. No matter; I was knocked up!

Almost as quickly as my thigh girth increased, invisible antennae grew out of my scalp and I started to notice every single preggers woman on the street. It seemed like the whole world was in bloom! Suddenly, strollers of every style and color were ubiquitous, tempting me in a buffet of varieties. Little onesies cooed from their store window perches, shrunken Tretorns were purchased for the tadpole within, and every child's name called out by mothers on the street hung in my brain for consideration like the crisp clash of cymbals; I like Ike! Cute as a little boy, hot as a guy, and cute as an old man again!

This would be fun, this mom thing, yay!

And then . . .

I ran into Patient Zero. No, not the Canadian flight attendant who porked his way into posterity. Her. The woman who would win the gold medal were name-dropping an Olympic sport, who answers, unprompted, *"Valentino!"* if you say you like her jacket, who weaves her colleges and clubs into every convo. It was like the Tourette's syndrome of the insecure. "Yeah, in New Haven, you know, *at Yale,* and then in grad school in Boston, well, outside Boston, in Cambridge *at Harvard,*" etc. etc. So there I was, bump in blossom, when she spied me.

"What are you having? When are you due? You know my son got a *ten* on his Apgar test. *Ten!* And they usually only give nine. But he got ten."

I'd been reading *What to Expect* and other tomes, so I was loosely familiar but not 100 percent sure. "Wait . . . aren't those, like, whether your heart's beating and shit?" I asked.

"Well, yes, but *alertness* is *key*. My son was sooo alert. The nurses said they'd never seen a more alert baby. Never!"

Ah, and so it begins: Apgars now, SATs later. Always a yardstick, ever a measure. Perhaps in Texas it's cheerleading captain or in Alaska how many fish you spear, but in New York City it's schools and social stuff and dough. Which many of these women had in the bubble of the Neo–Gilded Age—their husbands all put the "douche" in "fiduciary." They all threw money at any issue, hiring consultants for walking, talking, peeing, pooing, and violin. No matter! I simply wouldn't let it get to me. Or so I thought.

The next ambush came at my baby shower, where a

whispering group of older moms told me a thing or two about a thing or two.

"Wait, you're not having a C?" one gasped, incredulous.

"Um, I m-mean, unless it's an emergency . . . ," I stammered.

"So you're doing it, like, *natural*?" another said, hand to chest in horror, accompanied by a grimace like the passed hors d'oeuvre she'd just sampled was a shit profiterole.

All eyes were on me.

"Well, no, not natural, I plan on having drugs, obviously," I replied.

"No, but, like, you're going to . . . give birth?" the first asked, face contorted. "No, no, no, no. Schedule a C. You get a blowout, you get your nails done, you go in, you get the private room, and you remain intact down there. Trust me, your husband will thank you for it."

I left considering these whispered warnings. Was I so out of it? Did people think I was like some hippie mama going into the woods and shitting out my baby? Was my vagina going to resemble the Holland Tunnel?

Cut to: obstetrician's office.

**Me:** I'd like a C-section. My husband will thank me for it.

**Her:** You're insane. I don't do that.

**Me:** But all these other doctors do it! Like Dr. S!

**Her:** Yeah, well, he slices around the Duke basketball schedule. I'm different. I let nature decide your baby's birthday.

Unfortunately for me, and my vagina, my daughter arrived a week late, tearing through me like a bowling ball on its way to a strike. Except for instead of a flying-pin cacophony, it was my ear-piercing shrieks from hell. Because I was obeying the nurse who told us not to come to the hospital before the contractions were five minutes apart or we'd be sent home, I sat at home for hours like an asshole with a stopwatch timing my spazzing ute. At five minutes, I gathered my shit. By the time we got to our lobby, they were four minutes apart. By the time we scored a cab, three.

Wails. From the whale.

We stormed up to the delivery ward to find that there was a wait for the anesthesiologist so there was no epidural to be had. And get this! No birthing room available. My doctor was mortified and apologizing profusely as they wheeled my IV-harpooned ass into . . . wait for it . . . a supply closet. Yes. Stacked with boxes upon boxes of latex gloves.

"Um, I'm sorry, but am I in Ecuador?" I asked my husband.

I was later given morphine mid-pushes but I felt everything and was unpleased (read: RIPSHIT).

Oh, and by the way, my doc took such pity on me that for the next two kids I got my epidural in the fucking parking lot.

They took Sadie, demucused her, put her under that French fry warmer thing, and handed her to me in a blankie, pronouncing her Apgar a nine. (Boo! There goes Princeton!)

We brought her home in the "going-home outfit" soon to be splattered with doody, so why I didn't just go with Old Navy I have no idea. The first four months I was underwater. Like Brooke Shields before me, down came the rain. Except I literally sobbed at fucking commercials. There was one for Volvo where the daughter is at ice-skating class and keeps falling on her *tuches* and then comes out and Mom has the Volvo running outside with the ass warmer on. Now that's maternal love! Niagara Falls. I personally raised the stock of the parent company of Kleenex those first months. Especially because of the incessant pressure to nurse when the truth was, I didn't like it. People adore the symbiosis of mother and child and the bonding, but the truth was I wasn't breast-fed, and moms and daughters couldn't be more bonded than I am with my mom. My nips bled, the pumping made me feel like I was hooked up to a Frankenstein machine or, worse, that fat albino's below-tree-root death machine in *The Princess Bride*. I hated thinking of my baby as the Six-Fingered Man torturing me, so I bagged after six weeks. "Shame on you!" one beeyotch literally said to me, complete with pointer finger in my face. "You know it makes them *smarter*."

I knew right then and there I had to block out all the sudden advisers. My kid was only two months old and already a battery of people had given me their lists of things I "must do," from buy special toys we all somehow survived without to use $40 baby moisturizer. It was in this next year that my friends aligned in two camps—the ones who didn't have kids (my real friends) and the new breed of Supermom whom I met through my daughter. It was from this element that I learned the countless ins and outs of parenting.

**Comment:** "You give her food from a jar? Oh. We only serve all organic; we boil down a butternut squash from the farmer's market and puree it, and Allegra and Tabitha devour it!"

**Accompanying look:** As if I'm filling my kid's bottle with Coke and feeding her fried dough.

**Comment:** "You cannot use a pacifier at eighteen months. No, no, no, no, no, too old. That's lazy parenting. It causes speech delays."

**Accompanying look:** As if my kid looks like Hannibal Lecter with an enormous sucky mask and will be mute for the rest of her life because of it.

**Comment:** "You *must* do this playgroup: we have a PhD in child psychology come and we meet at different people's apartments, and it's like three or four grand but the babies are so advanced and it's worth it for the school process."

**Look when I politely decline:** Incredulity that a mom could be so uncaring about her child's brain development.

So I began to notice there was a breed of hypercompetitive type-A mothers whom I dubbed the Momzillas. I had my next book idea. Now I just had to get them to keep talking so I could harvest some material.

Cake.

I immersed myself in their scene, listening to diatribes on the choking hazards of nonsliced grapes or the merits of teaching Mandarin at age two. I lived my life gleaning conversational gems I couldn't have dreamed up for fiction. In fact my editor said I might want to tone down some of the over-the-top scenes and was floored when I informed her that the ones she had singled out were all 100 percent true.

When I signed up Sadie for our first Mommy and Me class, she was tooling around the room with her diapered bum, unable to sit down. As the teacher walked in, all the other moms quietly assembled in a circle on the floor.

"Sadie, honey, come here," I said, tapping the carpet next to me. "Come sit down Indian-style."

*Gasps.*

Literally no fewer than three bejeweled hands went to their respective throats.

I felt that seventh-grade tsunami of panic that I was being talked about when I saw two moms whispering while looking at me, i.e., making the international gesture for "We're talking about you." But see, it wasn't middle school, so I looked right back at them with a warm smile and said, "Is something wrong?"

They looked at each other. One grimaced and the other, caught off guard by my question, pursed her lips and leaned forward.

"Sorry, it's just, no one really says that anymore. It's not politically correct for the children."

What, "Indian-style"?! You're fucking kidding me. It's not like my apartment is full of cigar-store headdress wearers and I'm sitting there in a Redskins jersey greeting people by holding up a palm and saying "*How.*"

The other mom leaned in, throwing me the parenting lingo life raft. "It's called crisscross applesauce."

Oh. Okay . . .

"Sadie, come here please and sit down crisscross applesauce."

My husband and I had a good laugh that night about it, but not nearly as hard as we did the following week at a black-tie benefit for the American Museum of Natural History. Our friends Dana and Michael invite us every year, so we blow the dust off the tux and dress and hit the 'zeum in a glam night of people-watching and dining under an enormous whale. The cocktail hour, though, was in the main hallway, filled with life-sized dioramas of cave people with hairy boobs and animals about to pounce. I was click-clacking down the marble floor on my heels when I saw the Indians. Full feathers, drums, and a faux fire. They all sat around the sham flames with their legs crossed.

"Look, sweetie," Harry said. "The Native Americans are all sitting around crisscross applesauce!"

In the end, I learned (and am still learning) to swallow the unsolicited instructions and comments made by the Experts (moms with older kids) with a boulder of salt.

Because I have such an amazing mom, my instincts have generally led me in an okay direction and I feel aiiiiight. There have been a couple snags along the way, and I'm anything but conventional.

For example, at pickup one day when Sadie was three, the teachers, stifling a smile, informed me that my little smocked-dress-wearing daughter said the F word.

Mildly mortified, I asked for more detail.

"Well," said the teacher, "Charlie told her that her dress was hideous and she told him to fuck off."

"Oh, okay, well, she used it in the right context then!" was my reply.

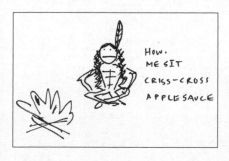

I probably should have been way more horrified and punished her in some way but the truth is (shhhh!) I secretly dug it. My kid wasn't going to take shit from anybody. So glad that apples don't fall far from trees. Crisscross applesauce is so much more fun that way.

# 12

# My Top Ten Most Blush-Inducing Moments of Motherhood (Thus Far)

10. Ivy asking someone at the supermarket checkout when the baby was coming. It was a dude.

9. My son, Fletch, at eight months, getting a baby doll in music class and proceeding to dry-hump it, causing one mom to suggest I film it and submit it to *America's Funniest Home Videos*.

8. On a crowded airplane, baby Ivy having a very bad Code Brown, the up-the-back kind. It was so fucking gnarly that when I walked her down the aisle passengers gasped as if in need of military-caliber gas masks.

7. Having Sadie ask the father of a girl in her class if he was her grandpa.

6. Fletch hitting so many kids, we started calling him Osama bin Kargman.

5. Sadie refusing to walk down the aisle as flower girl at a friend's three-hundred-person wedding.

4. Ivy announcing in a quiet restaurant that she has a "*big big doody.*"

3. Fletch projectile-vomiting Similac onto Mommy's friend's silk dress.

2. Sadie telling an older heavyset man with a long white beard that he looks "exactly like Santa."

**. . . and the number one most blush-inducing moment . . .**

1. On a packed JetBlue flight, having Sadie say (loudly), "Mommy, when the plane goes up, up, up in the sky, the wheels go up into the plane's vagina!"

Ahhh, the humbling job of motherhood. You can try to be prim and perfect with matchy-matchy sibling outfits, the hair bows, the table manners, the polished smiles for the holiday card. And just when you think you can exhale at a crowded birthday party because your kids are fabulous, one smashes a chocolate-frosted cupcake on another's white dress. Or pushes a tot in a bouncy castle. Or dances Hannah Montana–style . . . to organ music at a friend's christening. Sadie used to dance so provocatively, I used to say she was four going on whore.

We can be the most preened and controlled adults, and even the most anal of us are simply forced to let go and surrender to the Fisher-Price explosion of pure chaos. In the preparent years, when a kid spazzed in a crowded theater, threw peas in a restaurant, or smacked his mommy, I just told myself what people have been telling themselves for millennia in order to propagate our fine species of *Homo sapiens*: when I have kids one day, they will never do that!

Oh, what a difference a broken water makes.

When the stork arrived with my oldest, Sadie, I couldn't help but think she was the most perfect creature ever spawned. And of course all mommies shine their rose-colored lenses upon each of their babies as they innocently babble and roll and coo. And then . . . you get to know them. First of all, let the record reflect that I adore my kids. They are a spunky, quirky, colorful bunch and I relish our time together. They are a wacky crew full of incredible observations, big hearts, and electric smiles. And when I'm bummed or tired or stressed, their little arms around me in delicious hugs are the Hello Kitty or skull-'n'-crossbones Band-Aid on all that ails me.

And yet, of course, no kid is perfect. And by the way, if they were, they'd probably be boring nose-picking losers later. Our edges make us what we are, natch. Who doesn't love a little sass and spice? But what about when that spice gets ratcheted up to the level of, say, a glob of wasabi?

Take, for example, the list above. Allow me to mention that if need be, I could probably do a top 100 list. Maybe

David Letterman should hire me. This was easy! But when I think about some of the moments that made me blush, I realize that, sure, they can be cringe-inducingly embarrassing, enough for me to press a Dr. Evil button and get sucked through the floor, but they can also be . . . lovely. Here is one example.

When Sadie "graduated" nursery school, they literally had a whole rooftop ceremony complete with "Pomp and Circumstance" playing from an iPod dock. The children lined up at the base of the stairs leading to the super-tall jungle gym. The parents were all in rows opposite the looming apparatus, cameras ready, grins wide. The head teacher then read each child's name. The child was to climb the stairs, walk to the tippy-top of the long slide, and slide down. At the base of the slide was the assistant teacher who gave them their little diploma to fête the milestone. Applause ensued.

Kid after kid slid down to spirited clapping. It truly was the cutest thing ever, a brilliant idea to cap off their little careers as toddler students. Then came Sadie's turn. She walked up the stairs, and my husband, Harry, and I were poised clutching the digicam with pride.

"Sadie Grace Kargman," the teacher said.

I drew a breath excitedly as my little munchkin got to the top. But then . . . she didn't slide down. She just stood there.

"Come on, Sadie, sweetheart!" said the teacher encouragingly after a few seconds.

Nada.

"Honey, come on down!" she coaxed again.

I could feel the stares of the parents as they started to turn each of their blond primped heads to look at us. While they all loved Sadie, they knew she could be a total spitfire, prone to clowning around, shaking her ass, saying "vagina."

"Geez, she's a handful!" a mom in a shoe store once said to me, shaking her head after a little whiny outburst over M&Ms.

Harrumph. You know what? I fucking hate that expression. Handful? Yeah, bitch, a handful of flowers, of Barbie shoes, of blond curls, of M&Ms. There's no more vulnerable feeling than the suspicion your kid is being judged.

"Slide on down, kiddo!" the teacher said, a tad agitated.

Probably only thirty or forty seconds passed but they seemed like forever. My heart was throbbing, my husband was sweating, and just as I was about to draw breath to call to her myself, she casually strolled across the top of the jungle gym deck away from the slide over to the fireman's pole and shot the fuck down like a total badass.

That's my girl.

One of the mothers commented, "That's Sadie! She always has to do it her way!" with a saccharine smile. I wanted to bash her face in. *Hell, yeah!*

Look, I was nervous and even maybe a tad blushy at first that she didn't follow directions. Kids are taught to do what they are told, obviously. Still, it was a weirdly great moment. That pole was high and she had total balls to do it her way. The assets that are wonderful for life are not the ones that are wonderful for grammar school. When we're adults, aren't we supposed to go outside the box, break the chain, and have some fucking cojones? Why should I have been embarrassed? What she did was actually pretty damn cool.

So when I think about it on a macro level, I sort of turn a little mental page in the Mommy Manual. Sure, I feel terrible if my kids are freaking on a packed flight, but really, will I ever see these people again? Why sweat a liter and feel the stress hormones coursing through my veins? Why add wrinkles to my already grooved forehead over a bizarre goody-two-shoes mommy comment, a thrown object à la Russell Crowe, or some whiny behavior? They're *kids*!

my daughter Sadie's joke (age 7)
Can't decide if I'm HORRIFIED
or proud...

Q: what did the butt cheek
say to the hole?

A: hey, neighbor!

Deep in my gut, I know one day, when my little nuggets are older and have their wits and manners hammered into them as parents and society demand, I will feel wistful about all those inappropriate comments, the unusual hues of an off-color observation, and the unpredictability of a chaotic life. I will long for the pulse pounding that accompanies their innocent social blunders, their lack of edit buttons, their blissful lack of awareness. I will miss blushing.

# 13

# Proposal to Essie Nail Color ~New~ Names!

*To the Namer in Chief, Essie Nail Colors*

*Hello!*

*As a longtime fan of your shades o' polish and their funny names, I thought I'd propose a few others, free of charge!*

*Petite and Perky*

*Bathing Beauty*

*Hamptons Hot Tub*

*Asspen*

*Backseat Blow Job*

*South Padre Island Orgy*

*Duplexxx*

*Stiletto'd Slut*

*Janie's Got a Gun*

*Cock Gobbler*
*Virgin Vamp*
*Booze Cruise*
*Hummer Holly*
*Twilight Temptress*
*Battered Wife*
*Seductive Sally*
*Gstaad Roadwhore*
*Gondola Fondle*

*Sincerely yours,*
*Jill Kargman*

# 14

# Right Address, Wrong Apartment

Living in a fourth-floor walk-up with a small child is no easy feat. Now add some rodents and fraternity-boy neighbors and you can start to see what my first two years of motherhood were like. When the movers put the boxes down and left, Harry and I looked at each other over my swollen belly.

"Our first apartment as a family," I said, looking at the fresh coat of pale yellow paint in the nursery for the baby whose sex we didn't know yet. I know, so annoying. I hate when people do that now. "One day we'll leave here and miss it . . ."

Wrong.

First off, let me explain that while it was a very nice location—Seventieth between Lex and Park—it was also the rat capital of New York, after Chinatown. As any Upper East Side dog owner who does late-night strolls will attest, the block is teeming. The Mellons' garden? Undulating with bodies. The summer months, especially, are a carnival of crawlies, feasting on the refuse from Corrado bakery on the corner and the former falafel joint downstairs. (By the way, the falafel smell wafted to my pregnant nostrils, causing much upchuckage. As my dad says, it's called falafel cause it makes you feel-awful.)

But lemme go back. We found the apartment not through a Realtor or even online but from a serial-killer-scrawled ad taped onto a phone booth. That's right, a phone booth posting, back when there were phone booths, complete *avec* those scissor-sliced tabs you can rip off and call. It seemed too good to be true, a spacious full floor of a town house for a ridiculously bargain-basement price.

As we climbed up the steep stairs for the first time with the owner, we noticed that the third-floor apartment had full-on crime scene police tape covering the door.

"Whoa," I said. "Was there, like, a dead body in there?"

The owner laughed. "Hahahaha! No, no, just some

bad tenants who didn't pay the rent and they've been evicted."

"Oh, sheesh!" I replied. "Glad they're out!"

After three months of no *Law & Order* tape removal I started to get a bit suspicious. One morning on the landing, I met the woman on the top floor, a lawyer who worked all the time, and asked her about the derelicts in arrears on the third floor.

"Um, is that what they told you?" she asked with a raised brow.

"What, about the people not paying and getting evicted?" I asked, confused.

"Yeah, no, that's . . . not the real story."

I decided to walk with her to the subway.

As it turns out, the people downstairs were not what had been described. The apartment was, in fact, a brothel. A full-on Upper East Side whorehouse filled with Eastern European hookers who serviced local guys.

"*W-what?*" I stammered.

"Oh yeah, I had my buzzer going all night long with drunk guys coming for a blow job. All these Fifth Avenue Wall Street types with three sleeping kids and the wife at home would say they were walking the poodle. I swear, some nights I'd come home and there were seven dogs tied to the banister pissing themselves while Daddy got head upstairs."

See, you can't write this shit. I was obsessed. As it turns out, fiber-optic cables had been installed to observe the operation and after a while there was a full police raid complete with handcuffing of Svetlanas and their johns. My neighbor said she and her teenage kids looked aghast from their fifth-floor window as the drama went down and half-naked girls—literally wearing boas—were led into waiting cars.

HA!

I tried 69 once just to say I did but couldn't stop laughing.

Then she dropped the bomb: our landlord was also indicted. He was in on the whole thing. In the coming weeks a police document was taped on the front door. My neighbor and I took it down and read it, jaws on floor. The state seized the space (which is why there was the police tape) and served the owner with a packet of countless charges. The packet included the price list: $800 for sex, $600 for a beedge. We were giggling but I was horrified.

I gave birth to Sadie a few months later, and as if I wasn't getting little enough sleep already, we got our first three A.M. horndog buzzer the one time she appeared to be sleeping.

"Hi, the password is four-one-one," a male voice slurred.

"Excuse me?" I yelled into the intercom, heart pounding.

"The password. It's four-one-one. I wanna see Josie."

"Oh fuck," I said to Harry. "It's a john." He ran to the window, where you could see whomever was on the stoop.

"Holy shit, he's wearing a tuxedo," Harry said. "The bow tie's untied. And he's wearing a wedding ring!"

I pressed the button to talk to our late-night 'truder.

"Let me tell you something," I said. "I've got the four-one-one for you. Josie's gone, so go back to your wife!"

We looked at each other, eyes wide, and I ran to the window. We watched him grumble disappointedly down the steps back toward Park Avenue.

Two weeks later, I heard some commotion downstairs. I took Sadie on my hip to scope the sitch. Two guys were cutting the bolts on the door to the brothel and opening it up. Somehow the landlords paid whatever fine had been levied and wriggled out of the charges. Now they were getting ready to redo the whole apartment and get some new tenants to cough up cash for them.

I looked in the door-way. It looked like some kind of Italian bordello: lavender paint, a velvet rococo settee, and a coffee table with *Jugs* magazines spread on it.

"Can I check this out?" I asked the contractor. "I'm obsessed."

"Sure," he said with a shrug.

I walked in and saw they'd set up each of the four bedrooms as a series of stalls with twin beds. On each headboard were scarves tied onto the posts and the bedspreads were cheesy pastel rumpled linens. I almost gagged thinking people were streaming in getting their rocks off next to other pairs on the other sides of the flimsy screens that separated the stalls. *So* gross. I mean, couldn't they hear the other people's moans and sighs? Vom.

I left within thirty seconds and needed to loofah my entire body. I felt so disgusting I couldn't deal. But over the next few weeks the whole place was dismantled. The furniture was removed, an industrial cleaning crew came in, and the whole floor was given a gleaming-white fresh coat of paint. When brokers began showing it, I asked to take a peek. I was astonished to find it was gorgeous. The once purple moldings now looked beautiful and they had way higher ceilings than we did. *Maybe we should move in,* I thought. *It would be kind of fun to live in a place with such a storied past.*

But it was too much of an effort—I mean, packing and unpacking is the world's biggest hassle; whether you're moving across town or downstairs, the headache is the same. So we opted to stay put.

Then the frat boys moved in. Four roommates, all analysts on Wall Street. They slaved during the week and then went fucking shithouse on the weekend. They rolled kegs up the stairs and threw ragers that went until dawn.

One afternoon, I knocked on the door and tried to

make nice with the sweet Tom Hanks–y one who had a serious girlfriend in Texas and was the mensch of the gang. I explained we had a baby and if he could please keep it down we'd be so so grateful. On my way out, I smiled and said, "You know the story about this apartment, right?"

They hadn't heard. I then regaled them with the whole history. There was a lot of high-fiving as if they could make a huge deposit into their spank banks if they were privy to what had gone on in there. If only their exposed brick walls could talk.

But our little bonding sesh didn't help with the nice neighbor thing. They were so dickish, in particular the bitter schmuck named Matt who played guitar (badly) for his gal pals, whom I spied starting their walks of shame as I left for my morning coffee with the BabyBjörn.

The last straw was the Middle Eastern joint downstairs. When our landlord let them move in (after promising on our tour that the space would definitely not be rented to a food place) it was during the summer months when I was still pregnant. Now the next summer's heat was upon us and 'twas the season for rats.

The first summer they were open they were relatively

clean (though the stench sickened me), but as the months passed they became increasingly cavalier about chucking their waste on the street outside in poorly tied bags. Soon the critters came. Tons. And they made their way into our building. One day, I came downstairs with a bag of Code Brown diapers and opened the garbage room door. There, staring at me and my Björned baby, was a cat-sized rat. The tail alone must've been eight inches. I screamed so loud Sadie burst into tears and I ran outside hyperventilating. That night, I announced to Harry that we were out of there.

We packed up and headed for the place that's now our home. But we know it was folly to think we'd miss our old haunt where we brought Sadie home from the hospital. I drive by now, wondering who lives there, wondering if, on occasion, a penguin-suited drunk buzzes for a BJ or if they spy the occasional rat despite the falafel store's exodus (it now houses a fancy jewelry store). I'd love to meet them and tell them what went down, share with them the story of their nondescript New York apartment. Maybe one day they'll get the 411.

# 15

# Thirty-four and Holding

For the first chunk of my adult life, I lived by a simple mantra to solve any problems that arose through the cracks in the Jill pavement. And it goes a little suh-in' like this: There Is Nothing That a Glass of Red Wine and a Blowout Can't Fix. Mommy's tired, crack that K Syrah! Mommy looks like ass, get a cheapie wash 'n' style at Jean Louis David, the McDonald's of hair care. (Like those golden arches, it hits the spot!) My locks, like the fries, are straight and shiny. But unlike fast food, fast hair leaves you beaming instead of barfacious, and without the violation of food rape. I used to say I was bulimic but without the purge part. I actually tried, after a couple over-the-top Thanksgivings, to pull the trigger, once going so far as to shove a pink toothbrush down there in epiglottis territory, but no such luck. I don't have the gag reflex maybe. Thank god, says my husband.

That was the cure to what ailed me, precisely *one* glass of *vino rosso* and a defrizzed noggin. Instant bliss.

But then . . . motherhood began to take its toll. I started to see why Kate Winslet was shoving a Dyson up her ute in the 'burbs in *Revolutionary Road*. I told my hubby to fucking DROP IT with the conversations about a fourth child, that I could barely handle my three. I told him there was a red opaque Ghostbusters sign on my uterus and that no womb with a view was available for a tadpole tenant. And if he didn't quit bringing it up, the DO NOT ENTER sign would migrate to my vag and I'd start scoping eBay for a vintage chastity belt. Wait, is that redundant? Yeah, I guess; it's like saying "vintage typewriter." Or "assless chaps." Anyway, I totally froke one day when I thought I was knocked up. I took a pee test literally on a playdate and confessed the reason for my long bathroom break to the mom, Eeling.

"It's negative. Thank the fucking *lord*!" I said, elated.

She high-fived me but then grimaced and looked at me knowingly.

"Is there a small part of you that's a little bit sad?" she asked.

*"HELL TO THE NO!"* I swore, hand to god. I would have spazzed. I know it's a "miracle" and a blessing and whatnot, but holy shit, I would have been in a one-way car service to that *Girl, Interrupted* place. Why? Because I had this strange sense, at thirty-five, that I was starting to lose my marbles. They were spilling out and rolling all over the floor in all different directions. And I didn't know what the fuck to do.

It began when I went to Frédéric Fekkai for what I thought was a trim of my bottom-of-boob-length hair.

"Can I ask how old you are?" Stefanie the stylist asked me.

"Um, thirty-five, actually!" I said sheepishly. "Just turned. Kind of freaking, total hagatosis maximus," I added in my best Latin.

"'Kay . . . ," she said, putting her long Liv Tyler–y fingers through my stringy hair, which my mom tells me looks like "wet linguini" when it's too long. "You know, I'm thinking we should really . . . cut it. Like chop," she said.

"Like how, like more than two inches?" I said, eyes bugging out like Rodney Dangerfield's.

"Well, your style is cool, like your clothes, your earrings, but . . . honestly? Your hair doesn't go with the rest of you. Your hair actually makes you look older. I think it would be really chic and really fresh to have an angled bob."

Pause.

Mac rainbow wheels spinning for a moment.

Okay, so . . . not even top of boob. Not even collarbone, which I hear is the new shoulder. Not even shoulders. Fucking *bob*?!

I took a deep breath. It's just hair, right? Exhale. Fuck it.

"Done. I trust you." I shrugged coolly with the confidence of a badass woman who isn't attached to looks 'cause I have bigger fish to fry. What a load of shit. I knew I was merely an actress in my little one-woman show. But I delivered my nonchalant line with Tony-caliber panache: "Let's do it."

So that is how I chopped seven inches off my hair. It was swiftly lopped to my chin without so much as a text to my husband.

When he saw, his jaw was on the floor and had to be lifted off with small cranes.

But not as much as when I announced that at thirty-five, I would be getting a tattoo.

My desire was sparked as a child; I was somehow attuned to inkage on other people and my dad confessed he'd always wanted one. My mom, who was raised Ortho, never would have gone for it, but my Reform dad wore her down a bit, and by the time my brother moved to L.A. and got a bunch, they were fine with it. So fine, in fact, that on one trip, about ten years prior, we all spontaneously decided to get *K*s on our asses.

The four of us—Mom, Dad, bro, and I—wandered into Body Electric, home of Tommy Lee and the gang's tattooists, and the dude was just unwrapping a huge foil-encased steaming burrito.

"Aw, man, I just got lunch. If you come back in twenty, I can do ya."

"Okay, great, we'll come back in twenty!" my dad said enthusiastically.

And then . . .

*Bok bok bok bok bok!*

The Kopelman Klan chickened out in that mini time period.

Fast-forward to my thirty-fifth birthday and my brother and I decided it was time to fulfill my dream of being a BAMF. And that he would accompany me to the needle. But not on my butt or above my ass crack, tramp-stamp-style—rather on my back, like where Angelina Jolie has the coordinates of where her adopted Mohawk children were conceived or something. Above bra strap so that when I wore a black-tie dress it would show and I'd be all naughty and nice. Sugar and spice. Leather and lace. Velvet and ink.

Even though I am a grown-up, my mom vetoed it. But not how you think, throwing some kind of hissy fit; she announced that back tattoos were cheese and instead I should get it *on my wrist*. I explained to her that the back was kind of semi-sinful because I could cover it up when I chose to, but the very public wrist was a full-on plummet into scumbaggery for all the world and their country club pals to see. No matter, she said! Wrist somehow felt more dainty and delicate and feminine and sexy. Done. I would get a thread-thin ethereal, swirling letter *K,* for my last initial, both married and maiden.

Willie, my brother, came with me to Saved Tattoo in Williamsburg, where celeb tattoo artist Scott Campbell talked me down from freakage over potential pain. My heart had been pounding out of my chest all damn day in sonic booms that were so deafening I almost uncorked some vino, but I was informed that alcohol thins the blood and can cause a gusher. So yeah, no wine. Fuck me. How was I gonna get through this?

I followed Scott across the studio, passing huge ripped muscle guys lying on gurneys wincing in pain as their blood was dabbed away with gauze. Motherfuckercocksucker, I was so dead. Toast. These megabeefcakes were buggin' and li'l ol' me was getting my little wrist stabbed? Oh, jeez. I watched one (whose tat was snakes crawling in and then out of the two eye sockets of a skull) actually get up and walk it off, he was in such tortured agony. I almost shat. I somehow suspected that I would be one of those losers who end up with just a small dot because I wouldn't be able to take the pain and would give up. Willie looked me in the eye and told me that I could do this. I'll never forget it. I took a deep breath. My brother took my hand in his as Scott injected me. And . . .

"That's *it*?!" I marveled.

"Yeah, not so bad, right?" Scott said.

"Oh my god, these guys are all a bunch of lame-ass pussies," I said, jutting my chin toward the dudes weeping at the other stations. "This is nothing next to child-birth!"

Allow me to say right here and now that it's a good thing men don't have vaginas, because having a bowling ball cruise through a straw that barely holds a Playtex slender regular tamp is *so* much worse than some ink shot under your skin!

One word to all ye considering a tattoo but fear the stick: cake. It didn't hurt at all! Okay, maybe that's a lie; I mean, of course it hurt, but nothing like babies trashing your vag wall, so yay! Now I want more.

The preppy Lilly Pulitzer set shat twice on Nantucket, where I went later that summer. "Um, is that . . . *real*?"

"Yup!"

"Wait . . . like, permanent?"

"Uh-huh!" Yeah, that's usually how it works, Muffies.

I didn't get it to shock the preppies and separate the wheat from the edgy chaff, but it doesn't suck to sort through the varied reactions. Some of the most librarian stick-up-the-ass girls are the first to admit they've always wanted one. Others, of course, recoil in horrified disapproval, saying, "What will you do when your daughters want one?" And I tell them what I told my kids: "Get whatever you want. When you're thirty-five."

There will be no ankle butterfly or Grateful Dead bear on hip because I have made it clear that I changed as a person from teenhood and so will they. So knock yourself out! Once you're married with kids and know who you are. Sort of.

And, by the way, my kids dig it and Sadie even wanted my wrist for show and tell at school. I feared at first some of the yummy mummies would be mortified that I got it, but little by little foot vines and suns on hips were revealed to me, badges of a former life when they were following bands instead of applying Band-Aids.

But then the final symptom of what I now realize was my midlife crisis reared its head. My childhood of Friday-night Chinese food cartons and Crocket and Tubbs finally caught up with me: I needed to shoot guns. Immediately. Like once it dawned on me that I had the desire to feel the click of the trigger, I needed to sign up faster than a line of coke was snorted in 1980s Miami.

In my asexual bathrobe I call Grover because it looks not unlike skinned Muppet hide, I logged on to the West Side Pistol website. I filed for a background check, which obviously was spotless, perfect mommy angel that I am. I went in for my first lesson and fit in nicely, as my instructor John was sleeved in tats. I felt my wrist gave me street cred with the pistol-packin' posse. He took me in a back room, where he gave me the tour of the gun and gave me my "eyes and ears"—i.e., goggles for protection from flying shrapnel shards and giant noise-canceling muffs for the bang-bangage.

I reeled the target out to its beginner spot. BAM BAM BAM! I felt like I needed vintage Batman-style starbursts with the exclamations in primary-colored bubble-font blasts. BAM! KA-POW! SHAZZAM BAM!

Sorry for the self-horn-tootage, but I must brag . . . I rocked it. It was me and tons of older cops and I blasted that target like it was everything bothering me: diapers,

Momzillas, pressure, deadlines, cleanup, wrinkles, boobs at half-mast. BAM! Spilled wine. BAM! Crowded subway. BAM! BAM! Beeyotch on the school steps who told me I "look exhausted." BAM! BAM! BAM!

I felt like a million bucks. For the first time in as long as I could remember (or rather, since my friends Josh and Shoshanna's 1980s theme party), I felt high. I knew this was for me, and finally I had a sport I was good at. I was the shittiest athlete my whole life and now I finally aced something. Target after target was smithereens. One was a total 1970s-looking thug with too-tight trousers with a bulge in them, and he looked really rapisty. Well, I shot his ween clean off. No pinball-machine ravaging for me! Fuck you, asshole, BAM! Twenty holes marked where his paper dick once was.

I filed for my handgun license in New York City, which, BTW, is no small deal. Four visits to Police Plaza and laser fingerprinting, an investigator, the works. I bought a charcoal-gray Glock bag and my own eyes and ears.

It's not like I'd been wearing *Saturday Night Live* pleat-front Mom Jeans and JC Penney pastel-threaded tapestry vests, but for the first time in ages, I felt sexy and cool, not a mom but a badass with a killer shot. People still don't quite get why I do it, but to each her own. Some do Pilates; some go boxing at Punch; I pull the trigger, pulling myself to a calmer place as I do it. And somehow, as thirty-six dawns while I type this, I feel a little—just a little—bit more centered. Somehow all the changes of the past year have sharpened who I am, helping cement what I want to do in my limited spare time, helping me be happy, helping me hit the target of adulthood.

# 16

# Tumor Humor

While firing guns does make me feel like La Femme Jillita, nailing rounds of bullets into targets emblazoned with an angry rapist with a big hungry bulge in his pants, it doesn't take care of the crows' feet marching across my lined face. I was starting to feel extra old, especially when I looked at my mug in the mirror after waking up. Puffy, creased, spotted, tired. I'd examine each new wrinkle, cringing as I plucked a gray hair. As with all things in my life, I am black or white. Impulsive. Extreme. I went from my mirror to my address book to phone my dermatologist, one of the best in New York. I took the first available appointment.

"So I'm thinking," I said to the man who was used to just checking my countless moles, "I'd like to get some

Botox, please. On my elevens. The two vertical gashes above my nose where I seem to hold my stress. I need them gone. They're so deep I could canoe down them with my family."

He looked at me through his glasses, horrified. He took them off and stared at me, shocked.

"I would never, ever inject Botox," he said. "I'm a medical dermatologist. I could make a fortune doing it, but I don't feel like injecting poison in people's faces. If you really want this, you need to get what I call a scumbag dermatologist."

I shrugged.

Okay!

So I found one. A pal of mine has six kids and got the 'tox; she looks earthy and pretty and so not plastic. Sold. She made the intro to Dr. Anita Cela, who was not at all a scumbag but rather a cool, attractive, un-Barbie New York mom with a thriving practice, chill bedside demeanor, and relaxed, natural vibe. She instantly put me at ease as I explained I was craving a fountain-of-youth fix to freeze the wrinkle sitch. It was not only the number 11 engraved by the burn of time but also four perpendicular lines above it that looked not unlike Freddy Krueger had dragged his razor claw across my forehead.

After a series of the tiny shots, which were little leagues next to my tattoo, I might add, I was finito. I was getting up to get dressed when I had a quickie last question for sweet Dr. Cela, who was already walking out. "Do you mind just taking a quick peek at this mole?" I asked. "My other doctor said it was fine, but it keeps bleeding."

"How long has it been bleeding?" she asked, coming to check the spot on my right upper thigh.

"Oh, like on and off for over three years," I said blithely.

"Really?" she asked. "Your other doctor didn't want to biopsy it?"

"Well, no, I mean he saw it three times and he said it's benign and that it's in a highly trafficked area and that it may have been rubbed by a garment or something."

"Hmm. Well, it looks totally benign, but if it's bleeding, I'd get rid of it!" She told the nurse to prep and then sliced the fucker off. I didn't think about it again.

Then, a week later, in a deluge of biblical proportions, I was pushing Fletch in the stroller while holding a massive umbrella when my cell phone rang. It was my doctor with the pathology report. Not the nurse, but Dr. Cela herself. Uh-oh.

"Jill," she said in a grave tone, "I'm so sorry, but I'm afraid I'm calling with some very bad news." I stopped on the street, stunned, as my heart started pounding out of my chest like Roger Rabbit's. "You have a very rare type of skin cancer. I was so shocked when I got the pathology report that I called back the lab to have them double-check the results, explaining you were a young mother, but they confirmed the findings. You need to get to Memorial Sloan-Kettering right away . . ." She went on and I morphed into robot mode, barely hearing a word but nodding and recording the number to call and what I needed to do. It wasn't until a half hour later, when I heard my parents' voices, that I lost my shit and burst into tears. Luckily my mom had volunteered at the hospital for nineteen years and within hours of everyone scrambling I had an appointment for the next day.

My surgeon, Daniel Coit, who is the head of tumors at MSK Cancer Center, explained that they needed to take out the lymph nodes in my vag to see if the cancer had spread, plus obviously take out the whole area around the tumor, which was placed at stage 2 because it was growing into my leg beneath the mole. I was slated to go under the knife four days later. I looked at the surgeon's associate and said, "So, like, what are the chances that, like . . . I die?" He looked at his colleague then back at me, clearing his throat.

"Fifteen percent."

I *burst* into tears.

"I said one-five, not five-oh!" he said, surprised at my weepiness.

"I *know*!" I said through my tears. "That's still bad! I have three kids! That's one in six! Point something!" I froze. People around me went into action, sending flowers, notes, and chocolate, but I was in panic mode. I just couldn't imagine dealing with years of battling this crap of scans, blood tests, radical diet change (fourteen Sprites a week became one, and buh-bye to Britney Spearsian snack food, including a Cheeto-dust-free existence), and more vitamin horse pills a day than I have fingers and toes. As if I had time!

Four days later, I went in and was facing going under anesthesia for the first time in my life. I was freaked but knew people did this every day and it was no biggie. I just didn't wanna chunder. Before my surgery, I had to go for tests in Nuclear Medicine, where they injected a radioactive dye into the site and the nodes and I had to lie in a tube.

"Like . . . lie still?"

"Yes, totally still. You can't move or we have to start over."

"Okay, so, it's like twenty minutes?" I asked, recalling a thyroid scan I'd had years back.

"Nnnnno, it's seventy," the nurse said.

Sweat. Pouring.

"*Seventy minutes?*" I gasped. "Oh my god, I can't, I can't do it. *I CAN'T LIE IN THERE FOR SEVENTY MINUTES HOLY FUCKING SHIT!*"

The nurse calmly explained they would sedate me with a megadose of Klonopin and that that I'd be fine. I started breathing so heavily I feared I'd lapse into hyperventilation that would necessitate a brown paper bag, just like when I tried to show off in a camp color war minimarathon and collapsed in a red-faced wimpy mess.

I swallowed the pill and felt the beats of my heart speeding up rather than decelerating. I was shaking from the cold of the hospital creeping through my little gown and I thought I wouldn't have the strength to deal. And then something happened.

The door opened and in walked another patient for the same procedure. She was eight. I instantly felt so shitty and so loserish for freaking when this precious child—a second-grader two years older than my oldest daughter—was facing the exact same thing. In that moment, my whole world changed. Of course I always knew there were sick kids, but when faced with my own mortality I spun into self-protection mode and never realized how *lucky* I was that it was me and not one of my three children. I thought about this cute girl's mother, sobbing there in the claustro waiting room with tattered issues of *National Geographic*. I pictured it being me and how I would pray to switch places. So, see, my wish came true. It was me over my kids. And from then on, I never complained, never felt scared. Not even once.

Okay, except when I woke up and saw the eight-inch scar up my thigh. And that wasn't even the bad one—the vag one was way more painful an area, as the groin holds tender nerves, but eventually the pain subsided. (Thank you, Percocet! And Colace, for dealing with what accompanied the Percocet!)

And now as I face my first bathing suit season looking not unlike Sally from *The Nightmare Before Christmas,* I'm okay with it. Actually, better than okay—I weirdly dig it. It's a jagged badge of honor that shows how lucky I am. And it's a reminder that I need to slather sunblock on my kids like I'm papier-mâchéing them in zinc. Can't be too careful! And can't be too grateful. My vanity saved my fucking life. Thank the lord for scumbag dermatologists.

# 17

# Putting the Ass in Aspen

Weirdly, even though I don't believe in God, I still usually spell it G-d just in case I piss him off. Jews have this weird thing about not spelling His Name but meanwhile I text people "OMG" all the time, and once I stupidly e-mailed my mom "OMMFG" and she almost shat when I told her what it stood for. Oops. Sorry, G-d! You're so not a motherfucker!

Well, despite my agnostic Jodie Foster–in–*Contact* stance, minus the whole desire-to-travel-through-space thing, I must say I love me some Jewy songs. I go to temple most Friday nights and probably put the "sin" in "synagogue" when I say that I use it for peace, not prayer. I love the gorgeous sanctuary. I love the music. The cantor, Angela Buchdahl, has a voice that is so gorgeously spine-tingling it almost makes you believe in gifts bestowed From Above and whatnot. My rabbis are brilliant, so it's like a lesson, even if I can't buy burning bushes and seventy-year-olds getting knocked up.

Judaism to me is about soul and humor and warmth and food and family and our conspiracy to take over the planet. Just kidding. But I totally sometimes get how people think the Bernie Madoffs of the world are running rampant. Even I, as a proud Jewess, sometimes understand how peeps might think the bewigged Hasidic wives patrolling Madison look kinda sickly and the well-preened BlackBerrying Japs with their Escalades and blowouts and six-inch Louboutins are stereotypes that are upheld for a reason.

But still I partake in all the normal holiday traditions, including the Passover Seder. In the past it was all about finding the Afikomen and scoring me some cizzna$h (I know, how Jewy of me), but now, in my old age, with little money-hungry tots of my own searching for the hidden matzoh, I just love the tradition. Namely the wine. Manischewitz tastes like Robitussin and I fuckin' love the shit. It's sickly sweet and goes right to your head and helps you deal with the looooong Haggadah until actual meal-time. Plus, let's not forget, the Exodus is some pretty heavy stuff, yo! Locusts? Death of the firstborn? Bottoms up, yo!

So last year it just so happened that the eight-day holiday's beginning landed square in the middle of spring break. We were with my in-laws, who took us to Colorado, specifically Aspen (which, while beautiful, is basically New York with snow). I spied all these yummy mummies from home decked out in heels at ski school drop-off while I was in my parka and robotron ski boots. These girls get blowouts in the *mountains*. It's simply too fancy-pants for me. I like being mellow. I like to hide. I like restaurants without a deejay spinnin' it. We're out west! Give me a big fucking moose head, not a Skeletor hostess with 'tude! I can get that back home! To top it all off, my mother-in-law announced that for Passover we would be having Seder at the (very upscale) Hotel Jerome. Oh no.

*The eleventh plague:* dinner with 150 *strangers.*

With white tablecloths! And a three-hour service! Holy shit. My kids would trash the place! *They'd better serve Manischewitz,* I thought.

I got the kids all dolled up in their cute outfits, trying

to explain that it was not a party but a service and they would have to sit still. We pulled up to the hotel and found a long line to check coats; already my kids had ants in their pants, and they were darting around the high-ceilinged lobby. I gulped, hoping to gracefully pull through the endless evening ahead of me. I looked at Harry and did a deep-breath-eye-roll combo, as if to say, "This. Is. Going. To Suuuuuuuuuuuuck."

I walked in to find hordes o' Jewsteins in a large bar-room with a thirty-foot ceiling, milling around, mostly the L.A. Hillcrest genre with black T-shirts and gray mullets that say, "Who, me, aged?" The two huge sets of mahogany double doors leading to the ballroom were closed and we were told they would open in an hour, which, like dog years, has to be multiplied when chasing three small children. I was going shithouse. *Oh, lordy, this is going to blow.* I got a glass of wine. I lost one of my kids, found him again, and then spied a few kids coming in with crayons and coloring books. Shit. I wish I had thought of that! But who thinks of that when it's a Seder? Then I saw that in fact a woman was handing them out! *Géniale!* We went up to her and saw that in fact they were Ten Plagues coloring books, complete with cheerful bubble font for each page. One of them said "Cattle Disease!" and the kids could color in the sideways dead cows lying on the grass. Good times!

I flipped through one to see if they would "go there" with the dead babies, and yes, there were little papooses with *X*s for the eyes. Insane. My kids had already settled down to coloring in their little locusts when all of a sudden, the doors burst open to the ballroom, revealing . . .

Purple and red lights, a disco ball, and *a full black choir in full robes* singing "My Girl," except it was "My God." "My God, my God, my God, talking bow-ooo-out my Go-o-o-d, my God!" I burst out laughing. After the Temptations cover, my temptation to bolt was quashed. This was actually mildly amusing.

Then we were led to our table and my jaw dropped. The entire silk quilted tablecloth was covered with rubber insects. Plagues! It was *hilarious*.

But there were also about twenty Ping-Pong balls. All over. Next to the wine, the bread basket, everywhere.

*What's with the fucking Ping-Pong balls?* I was thinking as my son grabbed one and promptly chucked it across the table.

"Oh my god"—I answered my own question as it dawned on me—"HAIL!"

FUCKING BRILLIANT.

I almost peed myself with delight when the lights went out and remixed music blared.

"*Lady Gaga!*" both my two- and three-year-olds chimed in unison. (No "Baby Beluga" or "Hot Potato" in Casa Karg! Screw the Wiggles and the Qantas plane they flew in on.)

I could barely tell what it was at first but then through the pounding bass and darkness I somehow made out the opening chords of "Poker Face." But it was slightly different. On two huge screens flashed images of all the Jewy celebs, from Amy Winehouse to Seinfeld to Gwyneth Paltrow, and the reworked song title was "Kosher Face."

"*K-k-kosher face my k-kosher face! I'm gettin' hot, for bagels and lox, sh'ma-ma-ma . . .*"

Midgulp, I did a full spit-take of Manischewitz and almost fell on the fucking floor. *You can't make up this shit.* Then they passed out the Haggadahs, which were in fact not three-hour tomes but rather a McService called 30MinuteSeder.com. Like literally the dot-com was in the title. Perfection. After the insta-Seder, the choir got back up and rocked out to some tunes, and then a deejay took over. The entire ballroom devolved into a huge bar mitz- vah *blowout*. We were shakin' ass in Aspen and I felt like a total a-hole for freaking out so much. I thought it would be a plunge into the seventh ring of Hades but it turned out to be pure heaven. We shimmied for two hours and did everything but the chair dance. It was insane. I howled laughing, pocketed some locusts for posterity, and left knowing that I would cherish it as the best Seder ever. I also took home the lesson that sometimes the things we dread the fuck out of turn out to be our most treasured memories. I so did not see that coming and whenever I think about it, this k-k-k-kosher face cracks a huge smile.

# 18

# Spinagogue

Not only do I abhor exercise, I also detest people who talk about exercise. These evangelists who preach about their latest fitness obsessions (Pilates, Gyrotonics, Ironman triathlon training, vaginal kegels) make my eyes roll into the back of my head. I live near the park so I always see these couples jogging together side by side, dude in gray tee, girl *avec* ponytail swinging to and fro, each with matching stripes down their legs, so twelve stripes between them. They huff and puff and run, boobs 'n' balls bouncing in sync, then go home, tear off the Adidas, and have athletic sex. And to that I say: ew.

Where's the feminine mystery? The red lips? The lace and garters? Okay, fine, so maybe in lieu of La Perla *point d'esprit,* I'm wearing Urban O boy shorts, which ain't zackly smokin', but *still*. Oh, and also, here is my lifelong theory. Ready? It's controversial . . .

Working out makes you fat.

Yes indeedy. *Look* at those women in Paris, all dainty with their lithe limbies and bony bods? Not a StairMaster in sight! I live across from an Equinox gym and I see all the smoothie sippers going in and out all day long and bouncing away on treadmills. Lemme tell ya something: they be beefy. My most hippo-esque state was when I did the New York marathon. When I exercised I used to go and eat a frying pan (no, like, seriously, served in the skillet) of mac 'n' cheese at the now-defunct Drovers Tap Room on Jones Street. It was seriously Frank Lloyd Wrong. Two thousand calories recommended by the FDA? That stands for *fuckin' dream away*! If you work out you could Dyson *twice* that easily! So back to my theory. Better to not work out and be thin. Like my mom. And my late great-aunt Laura. She was a rail and simply walked Manhattan, buying her fish at the fish market and cooking without fat-free garbage. Both she and my mom always ate three squares. Not chowing, just three normal meals.

Me? I was always a binger. I used to never feel hungry

at breakfast time, so by the afternoon I was like the ravenous Tuscan wild boars in *Hannibal* that ate Gary Oldman's burnt face off. But when I discovered the magic of breakfast, I lost like eight pounds. I was full by lunch and had a half a sammy or a yogurt and then normal dindin. And that was when I had the idea for my bestselling diet book! You wanna know what it's called? Okay . . . drumroll . . . *Eat Less Food*.

It would be just one chapter! One page, actually. After years of trying to get down to my birth weight, I am finally satisfied with what I am. I'm embracing my bod! I'm happy! So why oh why, then, would I fucking start exercising?

Two words: peer pressure. No, not really. But kind of. I've turned down cocaine and never smoked pot, but spinning class? Pass the bong. I did it.

It all began when my friends Tara and Alexis started their spiel. They were addicted. It was a studio called Soul-Cycle, which in fact produced its own tank tops that said OBSESSED, where the *O* was a wheel. They claimed I absolutely had to go, issuing a friendship subpoena. I blew it off. Then everyone else started buzzing about it: the scene, the

Escalades all parked outside, the tits on sticks BlackBerry-ing outside, the Russian model with the oil-oligarch boy-friend who sends her in his Maybach, the yummy mummy of three who ran off with the hot lesbian instructor, the works. I was semi-intrigued but still said hell to the no.

**Them:** *Why?!*

**Me:** Because I *hate bike rides*.

**Them:** It's so not like bike rides.

**Me:** How is that *possible*? *It's on bikes!*

**Them:** Because it's not! It's *pitch*-black with music blaring.

**Me:** What do you mean, like . . . it's dark?

**Them:** Yeah! Totally dark.

**Me:** Is the music any good or do they play torturous crap and then I'm trapped there?

**Them:** It's *totally* good! It's like going to a nightclub. It's *fun*! You don't even realize you're working out!

**Me:** You guys are such cult members.

**Them:** Okay, it's true. But it's a good cult!

Their sermons morphed into Charlie Brown teacher-speak after a while, but then a few weeks later my friend Marcie told me that she had booked an extra bike. She wanted me to come with her for her birthday, and she even dropped off a full outfit in my lobby. Shit. I had to go.

CUT TO: "Hi, I'm Jill, and I'm a SoulCycle addict."

I go four days a week.

I'm a Branch Davidian–level devotee.

"Huh?" you might ask. Well, you'd be echoed by a chorus of all who know me. You? Spinning? Yes. My husband was so freaked that he told me that if the me from six months ago Michael J. Fox'd here and met the me of today, she'd smack me across the fucking face.

"Who are y-you?" he stammered. "You hate people who exercise!"

"I know. I don't know what's come over me. I've . . . changed."

He literally thought I was going to reach up into my hair and reveal a zipper that I'd pull down my back to reveal my scale-covered alien body underneath. That I was actually the reptilian Martian that ate the woman he called his wife, as if my real self was trapped inside like John Cusack at the end of *Being John Malkovich*.

So how the eff did this transformation occur, you ask? Well, the girls were right. It's fucking fun. And not only that, unlike real biking (which I hate), you don't have to bake in the sun. Yes, you schvitz because it is a workout. But you don't have to watch where you're going, so you can close your eyes and listen to the music and zone out. If you did that on a real bike, you'd smash into a road sign. Or run over a fallen branch and go flying and break serious boneage. Or simply ride through doody. In the studio, I'm just still. And despite blaring music, at peace.

My first class was very intimidating. I was a bit freaked by the French-manicure set with their spray-on tans and boobies and BeDazzled wifebeaters with the studio's Helvetica Bold logo. One girl was bitching that her bike was "in Staten Island," i.e., the back row of four. Those bikes are considered less-plum placement and are also called the Weeds, as in "Damn, I'm on bike forty-six today, I'm out in the fucking weeds!" I started there on purpose because

I didn't want to be front and center, where they sometimes get into your face to pedal faster. There was some choreography I had to learn, like getting "out of the saddle" (riding standing up), and they keep yelling at you to "engage your core," which basically just means suck in your stomach. There's also a weights section where you hold little barbells and do curls for all your 'ceps (bi and tri). Within weeks my pipes were honed and even had a little Popeye bulge, but not grodily. The only problem with the lifting part is that the bikes are close together and I happen to have obscenely long arms. Think *Australopithecus*. They practically drag on the floor behind me. So I almost always bump my neighbor with a sweaty elbow and have to mouth out "sorry" over the Jay-Z/Journey remix. But I guess I'd rather have my long arms than those short stumpy ones like the freakish sister with baby hands that Kristen Wiig plays on *SNL* in the Lawrence Welk sketch. I also learned strong arms are called guns, as in "nice guns," which of course I dig.

And, like all good cult members, I roped in a newbie: my mom. Yes, I dragged Maman after all my evangelizing and made her accompany me. I got her Smartwater and clicked her shoes in the pedals for her and watched her go. The first time she panted and sweated and practically fell into an X on Third Avenue when we exited.

"It's like Singapore in there!" she vented. "In August."

It's true. It is fucking sweaty as a Russian bathhouse à la *Eastern Promises*. Minus the switchblades. (Though I'd take a knife wound to be near naked Viggo any day.)

"What about all the germs?" my mom asked. "Everyone's sharing all that air!"

True again. I sometimes ride the bike hearing coughs over the vintage Michael Jackson/P. Diddy combo and think of that scene in *Outbreak* where it switches into GermCam and follows someone's spraying saliva all through a crowded theater. But I ain't worried; Dustin Hoffman and Rene Russo won't be kickin' down the door to SoulCycle in hazmat suits any time soon. In fact, I happen to think a little 'teria is good for us. Just like pain or sweat or sore muscles. And by the way, despite my mom's complaints that she was going to keel over afterward and there'd be a chalk outline drawn around her spinning outfit, she called me the next morning to say she'd signed up for the next two days. See? Cult!

I don't know exactly why, but somehow, all the components come together in that room. It's not just about the music or the motions, it's . . . gosh, I am such a sappy-ass sucker, but . . . (gulp) the soul. And I don't mean like spiritual yoga bullshit where everyone says "om" and it smells like ass with Parmesan cheese. But it is a happy empowering space, a little safe nook where the only light is two flickering votives and the teachers' voices inspire you to ride your fucking ass off. Which, by the way, I literally did. I used to have this pocket of cottage cheese between thigh and ass that I called thass, and now it's *gone*. Like, vanished. It's a fucking miracle. And yet, I don't even do it for my ass, I do it for my head. Working and organizing three kids' schedules sometimes makes me feel like I'm playing a never-ending game of Tetris. I wake up with such a gut-churning pit in my stomach, because all those little pieces are raining down on me and I don't know what to do. I manage to reconfigure them and guide them all into place, snapping them exactly where they ought to go, but just when I have the satisfaction that everything and everyone is settled, a new storm of challenges starts falling down on me. All my worries, all the stress, all the pieces, they evaporate when I am breathing and moving my body faster than I knew it could go.

My teacher MB says you can't change your body without a little pain, so you need to "shred it" with each ride, pushing yourself harder. In the front row, no less! Any mother can sometimes feel like the living dead, but there in the darkness, deafened by beats, I feel more alive than ever. I'm not swallowing Kool-Aid any time soon but I have indeed joined the cult, and no FBI deprogrammer can ever throw a burlap sack over me and drag me to the woods to convince me to stop. Part of me always wanted to be a feminine, witty Edith Wharton or Brontë heroine, and those ladies would never sweat their sweet lace-wearing asses off, but guess what? Those delicate dames also croaked early. And I have so much to live for. No matter how challenging each new day's Tetris storm is, deep deep down, I enjoy the rain.

# Acknowledgments

I wish I could say the idea for this book came to me in bed at 3:00 A.M. or in the shower or in a spontaneous Bon Jovi Blaze of Glory, but all credit actually goes to my editor, goddess Debbie Stier: part life coach, part tech queen, part friend and blue ribbon/gold medal/plaque–covered chalice winner for Most Charismatic Person Ever. Your enthusiasm is infectious and encouragement a gift. Thank you, Debbie. So effin' much.

Mega shoutouts also to the whole new posse at Harper-Collins/William Morrow: Kathryn Ratcliffe-Lee, Christine Maddalena, Seale Ballenger, Lynn Grady, and Liate Stehlik. To Jenn Joel, überagent, agent, and possessor of best shoe collection ever, you rule. Thanks also to Clay Ezell, Nancy Tan, John Kotik, Aja Pollock, Steven Beer,

Mary Miles, and the incomparable Carol Bell and Barbara Martin.

*Merci mille fois à* Pamela Berkovic, *amie* and photographer who feared I looked too ugly on the cover. I told her I was trying to look funny, not pretty, but *chérie* thank you for allowing *les "eedeous" photos*!

My first reader, as always, was Dr. Lisa Turvey, who gave notes while nursing a newborn. Now that's fuckin' friendship. And to my other chéres: Vanessa Eastman, Jeannie Stern, Dana Wallach Jones, and Lauren Duff— this book couldn't have been written without you.

Thanks also to my other close friends and supporters who have helped me so much along the way: Trip Cullman, Michael Jones, Dan Allen, Laura Tanny, Tara Lipton, Alexis Mintz, the Heinzes, Michael and Marisa Fox Bevilacqua, Michael Kovner and Jean Doyen de Montaillou, Vern Lochan, Carrie Karasyov, Julia Van Nice, Robyn Brown, Jacky Blake, Lynn Biase, Kelley Ford Owen, Jenn Linardos, Marcie Pantzer, Jeanne Polydoris, Daniel Wiener, Abby Gordon, Jonathan Prince, Lisa Fallon, Konstantin Grab, M. B. Regan, Nick Oram, Erica Kasel, Rebekah McCabe, Andrew Saffir, Daniel Benedict, Richard Sinnott, and all the Kargmans and Kopelmans.

And to all those who tortured me along the way—thanks for the character building! (Assholes.)

Lastly to my kiddos and Harry: thanks for letting me work away on this—I love you so much. And to my mom, dad, and Willie: you three shaped how I see the everything and everyone, and I'm so grateful for all our stories.